D1049800

JUN 0 1 2016

Got Here As Soon As I Could

PRAISE FOR SARAH SMILEY

"Often funny and always humane, an unexpected voice in a world long defined by ironclad rules and abhorrence of emotion."—*New York Times Magazine*

"Forthright and honest, funny and smart."—*New York Times*

"An Erma Bombeck."—*Publishers Weekly*

"You can't help but be moved."—Carol Leifer, former writer for *Seinfeld*

"[An] honest nature, quick wit, and endearing personality." —*Military Spouse* magazine

GOT HERE AS SOON AS I COULD

Discovering the Way Life Should Be

SARAH SMILEY

Down East Books

Down East Books

Published by Down East Books
An imprint of Globe Pequot
Trade Division of The Rowman & Littlefield Publishing Group, Inc.
4501 Forbes Boulevard, Suite 200, Lanham, Maryland 20706
www.rowman.com

Unit A, Whitacre Mews, 26-34 Stannary Street, London SE11 4AB, United Kingdom

Distributed by NATIONAL BOOK NETWORK

British Library Cataloguing in Publication Information Available

Library of Congress Cataloging-in-Publication Data Available

ISBN 978-1-60893-576-5 (hardcover)
ISBN 978-1-60893-577-2 (ebook)

∞™ The paper used in this publication meets the minimum requirements of American National Standard for Information Sciences—Permanence of Paper for Printed Library Materials, ANSI/NISO Z39.48-1992.

Printed in the United States of America

CONTENTS

CONTENTS

CONTENTS

CONTENTS

Preface

The Way Life Should Be

My first eight years of motherhood can be summed up like this: I drove little people through stop-and-go traffic, from one end of a busy city to another, for planned activities and sports.

We were living in Florida, where my husband was a Navy flight instructor, and if I'd had a daily to-do list on my refrigerator, it would have included just one item: Fill up all the time. My objective was to be busy. The rat race of motherhood, fueled by parenting magazines and self-help books, had convinced me that my young boys needed to be busy to be happy. If they weren't signed up for organized sports by the time they were 3, I had failed. If they were bored, it was my fault. If they had a single moment of unstructured time, I was a bad mother.

We had a 6-foot privacy fence in our backyard, and sometimes I allowed my children to play out there—but only if I was nearby and supervising their activity. This made me feel, for a moment, that my kids were having a childhood with some semblance to the kind I had, where you found your friends when you found their bikes lying on the ground in someone else's lawn.

The reality, however, was that my children were imprisoned. They were imprisoned by my ideas of what makes a good mother and my notions about how many things in the big, scary world could harm them.

Then one day, the military moved us to Maine.

Nothing that you read above applies in Maine. It simply cannot. Maine is filled with miles of lakes and forests that refuse to contain its children. Maine doesn't have traffic, nor does it have what most people consider a "big city." Here, children still walk to and from baseball practice. They ride bikes. They kayak with their friends and explore untouched islands. They don't see their parents until dinnertime. They actually play pick-up games at the park—without adults.

At first, I felt like I was in a time warp. It was as if all the nostalgia of the 1950s, long ago gone from the rest of the country, had settled here. Life was untouched; childhood continued, as it had, for generations.

You feel this the moment you cross the bridge from New Hampshire to Maine. The night sky gets darker, the stars brighter, and the air, somehow, lighter. Just past the bridge, there is a sign: "Maine—The way life should be."

Eight years ago, I passed that sign with a car full of suitcases and children, having no idea how the state was about to change us. In Maine, my children were set free to have the kind of childhood I had always wanted for them.

This book is filled with newspaper columns I wrote during our first seven years in Maine. Taken together, they show how we first overcame the shock of this new culture (my oldest son went from a school with 14 kindergarten classes to a school with just 2) and then how we embraced it. Within these columns, I hope you will see glimpses of your own childhood or your children's. If you're a new parent, maybe you'll see a life you've dreamed of for your family.

But wait! Don't despair if you don't live in Maine.

It's true that Maine's environment makes over-parenting difficult. But at one point in our history, neighborhoods all over our country operated like Maine's do—with sidewalks, parks, and parents who are willing to let go and trust. There is a reason Maine is Vacationland and why thousands of families send their children to camps here in the summer. However, Maine's ethos needn't only be a respite from the world's fast pace and privacy-fence jungle. Maine's ethos used to be America's, too. And it can be again.

—Sarah Smiley
Bangor, Maine

FOREWORD
By Senator Angus King

HOW CAN YOU NOT LOVE A BOOK THAT INCLUDES THIS: "I've yet to find an unattractive side to Maine"?

But although Maine is the setting—and frequent protagonist—of the stories, the real star is life itself, with its humor, frustration (ask Sarah about the Padres mug), ups and downs, and abiding love for family and place. It's literally impossible to read these little portraits without smiling (okay, spare me the puns), nodding in recognition of a familiar situation, and frequently laughing out loud at some deft description of one of life's challenges or unexpected rewards.

Although light and fun, these stories are also stealthily serious—with messages about patience, forgiveness, growing, engagement, learning, yearning, and, yes, love. Sarah's obvious love for those often obstreperous boys and her sometimes hapless husband infuses the book with the gentle glow that makes it so memorable. (Why is it, by the way, that husbands are *always* hapless in accounts like this? I know to a certainty that if and when Mary writes on this topic, I'll get exactly the same treatment—alas, I'm afraid, deservedly so.)

Sarah's special skill is presenting the commonplace in a fresh light—inviting us to see the familiar through new eyes, eyes that are usually crinkled in a smile. I've unconsciously known for years, for example, that zucchini is inherently evil and bent upon world domination, but it wasn't until I read Sarah's account of her battles with this most persistent of plants that I realized the full extent of its malevolence. (One of my favorite stories for out-of-staters is how in Maine we only lock our cars in September. "Why September?" they ask. "Because if we don't, somebody will fill them up with zucchini.")

Finally, a note on the writing itself. It's wonderful. Here's a small example coming at the end of a paean to summer in Maine, which, as Sarah points out, is so precious because it is hard earned in the winter before—

"When winter comes, we will all forget the flies and mosquitos of summer. Sunburns will fade and also be forgotten. We'll only remember moments like this, floating in a kayak, watching the sunset and listening to a boy talk about life.

Oh, Maine. Seasons come and go in a moment, leaving only the beautiful colors of a sunset in our memory. Until the next summer.

Because unlike most things in life—childhood, baby laughs, our 20s—that come and then are gone for good, we can all cling to the promise that another fleeting Maine summer will come again."

That last sentence is so simple, yet evocative and dead-on that it could have been written by E.B. White—and I can't bestow much higher praise.

In short, this is a special book—one you can dip into at will, and when you do, the rewards will be generous. And besides, you'll even learn what a ramekin is; how cool is that?

INTRODUCTION

From Away

I WAS WASHING THE CAR AND WEARING FLIP-FLOPS, BE-cause that's what you do in February when you live in Florida. My oldest son, Ford, then 7, helped me with the garden hose. By "helped," of course, I mean that he and my middle son, Owen, 5, just sprayed each other. They were barefoot even though the pavement was so hot, sudsy water sliding off the car hissed as it hit the driveway. After living in Florida for almost 10 years, the only things that really phased us were: poisonous snakes, alligators and red ants. Especially red ants.

Our youngest son, Lindell, had just turned a year old the month before and was bouncing in a playpen under the shade of the garage.

I thought my husband, Dustin, was still at NAS Whiting Field, where he worked as a flight instructor for the Navy, and I didn't expect him home for several more hours. He never worked regular 9-to-5 hours, and especially not then, when he was nearing the end of his tour and beginning to train a replacement.

Sometime after 3 o'clock, however, Dustin's white Explorer pulled into the driveway. He stepped out wearing his green flight suit and looking tired from the day. He tousled each of the boys' hair and kissed me hello. He was going inside to change, because flight suits and steel-toed boots are a little too warm in February in Florida.

On his way past me, Dustin stopped and said, "Oh, you're not going to believe this, but the Navy added Bangor, Maine, to our list of options."

By "list of options," he meant the eight locations—now nine, with the addition of Bangor—where the Navy might send us next. By "our list," he was referring to the fact that the Navy likes to make families feel like they have some control over where they will move, when in reality, someone at the Bureau of Personnel, where the military gives people new zip codes, likely throws darts at a map. That person is probably blindfolded.

In any case, for the last month, Dustin and I had been agonizing over where we should move. Our options ranged from Washington State to Harlingen, Texas. I wanted to get back to Virginia, which I once thought was the Northeast and now know is actually the South. Dustin wanted to go anywhere that I'd be happy.

We made a list of our top six choices, because that was all the Navy had required, and kept it on the refrigerator. Just like naming a baby, each of us had veto power. If Dustin chose Harlingen, Texas, I was ready to veto the heck out of that. Our top two, however, seemed to be Pennsylvania and South Carolina. Bangor, Maine, was not even on the Navy's original, larger list of eight locations. Now they had added it as number nine.

Before Dustin could go inside that day, and while warm soap oozed from a sponge in my hand, I laughed and said, "Well, good thing we aren't putting Bangor on our list of six."

"Actually, I added it as number seven today," Dustin said.

"Oh, well, I veto it," I said.

You see, our deal was that Dustin would not submit his "wish list" to the Navy until we had both agreed on our top six locations. I knew there was no way Dustin would turn in our selections until we had first made it official at home.

"I kind of submitted the final list today," Dustin said.

I dropped my sponge.

"And Bangor was number seven—" Dustin's voice trailed off. Maybe he was already envisioning his night on the couch.

I stormed past him and into the house crying. Dustin followed at my heels saying desperately, "Sarah, I put it as number seven on a list of six. There's no way they will send me there. I just couldn't not include it."

Dustin's dad, Phil Smiley, actually was born in Bangor. His grandfather, Henry, was a tow-truck driver and Ford mechanic. The Smiley family lived in Bangor until Phil was 12, and then they moved to California. No one from Dustin's immediate family had lived there since.

"I hope you have fun living in Maine," I said to Dustin as I shut our bedroom door, leaving him on the other side.

"They aren't going to send me there," he said through the door. "You'll see."

Two months later, on April Fool's Day (I'm not kidding), I was in the bathroom blowdrying my hair when Dustin came home from work. I saw him in the mirror standing behind me with a kitchen chair in his hand.

"You're going to want to sit down," he said. "The Navy is sending us to Bangor, Maine."

Dustin's only explanation: "I must have been the only candidate who even listed Bangor. So even though it was my seventh choice—"

I immediately went online and found forums filled with people who live in Maine. "What do I need to know?" I asked. "Is it really as cold as I'm imagining?"

People's replies went something like this:

"You're moving here from Florida? You're going the wrong way!"

"You're going to hate it. I give you one winter and you'll be running back to Florida."

"I have six feet of snow in my yard right now."

(Note: I now know these are the things that Mainers say to keep this beautiful state all to themselves.)

I'm not going to lie; I was more than a little scared. Our family didn't even own windbreakers. I told Dustin that we would go (as if we had any choice), but I would not stay one day more than his 2-year commitment.

The children and I arrived in Bangor in August. School was starting the next day, and although Dustin was still finishing his job in Florida, I wanted to get the kids settled into their new home. We would live in Maine without Dustin for about two months. During those two months, the boys were sleeping with wool hats on their heads. Yes, even though it was only early fall.

We had moved from a place where even in October it was usually still too hot to wear most Halloween costumes. Owen even wore mittens and a hat for his soccer pictures in September in Maine. He was that cold. Unfortunately, I forgot to fill out the paperwork for the pictures, so the photographer posted this on Facebook: "I'm sending photos tomorrow, and I have everyone's information except one. Does anyone know who the kid wearing mittens and a hat is?"

The boys also had not ever seen snow before. I saw our neighbors' winter preparations—reflective poles along the driveway, teepees over bushes—and feared the worst. As wind chimes clanged and the temperatures dove, it was like winter was an opponent getting ready in one side of the ring, and we humans were doing our best to get ready in ours. Except, I wasn't getting ready, because I didn't know how. I had never heard of a roof rake, and I didn't know what ice dams might do to gutters. Winter had me right where it wanted me.

Already though, I was falling in love. Yes, even as I saw winter's impending doom on the horizon. It is correct to say I came to this state kicking and screaming, but almost immediately, something strange began to happen. I felt at home. I had never really felt at home anywhere else that my husband and I had lived, and I certainly had never felt at home anywhere so quickly. In those early months, I asked myself, "What took me so long to get here?"

I fell in love with the eclectic neighborhoods, filled with all types of people, which were so unlike the gated communities we had known in Florida, where everyone lives in neighborhoods with people like themselves, and then they hide behind six-foot privacy fences.

I fell in love with the open backyards and my elderly neighbor's line of laundry hanging in the backyard.

I fell in love with the sidewalks that were cracked and uneven, and which always made me think about all the generations of children before mine who had walked on them to school.

I fell in love with the schools that were built in the early 1900s and still in use today.

I fell in love with the cake store downtown and the woman who runs it, and the library, and the one-room bookstore on Central Street.

I fell in love with the way the air smells just before the leaves begin to change color, and how fall casts beams of warm sideways light onto the street.

I fell in love with all the neighbors sitting on their front steps who waved and said hello as we walked to school.

I fell in love with the tiny neighborhood school that has two kindergarten classes and where the principal knew my children's names and favorite football teams by the end of the first week. We had just come from a school where Ford's kindergarten class was one of 14, and when I checked him out of school, I had to verify his student number.

I fell in love with the people huddled over coffee at small shops downtown, and the way that everyone gave me directions like, "Take a left at the house that used to belong to the dentist, then go straight a ways, and turn right by the house where the man with 4 dogs used to live."

I fell in love with the police department that instead of towing my illegally parked car, came into the store and asked who owns it first.

And I fell in love with the way neighbors met in the streets and plotted against Old Man Winter and their next round against him.

Right before Dustin left Florida to join us in Maine, I called him and said, "I love it and I'm never leaving."

"What happened to 'two years and not a day more'?" he asked.

"If I leave this place," I told him, "I will spend the rest of my life trying to get back here."

"Well, wait until I get up there, at least," Dustin said.

"Yes, and then you'll see. Maine really is the way life should be."

It's now been seven years since the Navy brought us to Maine, and I am still just as much in love with this state as I was back then. Ironically, the one place that has ever really felt like home for me is the one place I can never actually call "home." I'll never be a Mainer; always "from away." But in the columns that follow, which were written from 2008-2015, I hope you will see how Maine became the only home I'll ever know. I wasn't born here. I wasn't raised here. I didn't even get married and have babies here. But I got here as soon as I could.

WELCOME TO MAINE

A LESSON IN LIQUIDS AND SOLIDS

THE HUMAN BODY IS 60 PERCENT WATER. SEVENTY PERcent of our planet's surface is covered in water. Every day, in order to live healthfully, human beings must replace 2.4 liters of water, taken from the planet, for their body.

The world, it seems, is kept in balance with water. Which might explain why my fence gate won't open in the morning.

At first I thought the latch was jammed. Kicking at the bottom of the gate, I reasoned, would probably help. It didn't. And then I realized something that blew my mind: My gate was frozen shut. Soon after, I would learn that my car door also was frozen shut and the windshield wipers were stuck in the down position. If I wasn't careful, my children, who had never seen snow until this November, might get so excited, they would lick the light post and freeze there as well.

Water posed a different kind of challenge for me when we lived in Florida. First, the water in the South comes in only two forms: regular and mist. Gates don't freeze shut down there. But leave a bottle of water in your car on a day when the temperature reaches 100-degrees, and you will find out what happens to water molecules when they get very hot: they create steam. Pour that water onto the concrete (careful not to let your bare feet touch the hot ground), and you will actually hear it sizzle.

This doesn't happen in Maine. I left a bottle of water in my car one day, and it froze, as did my container of foaming, waterless hand soap.

The South also has plenty of water that is in its regular, not-frozen form. Flowing water is everywhere: the beaches; the lakes; a pool in every family's backyard; the neighbor's concrete statue of a naked baby pouring water from a bucket; drainage ditches; the 2-foot crater in the side yard that never empties and by the end of summer is a pool of hot, steaming mud. Still, replacing those 2.4 liters of water in your body each day is quite a challenge when you live in the South because you are always sweating it back out.

This is why the stereotype of Southerners is that they have a large glass of iced tea, condensation streaming down the sides, in their hand. I miss iced tea. It's hard to come by up here. No one in their right mind wants more ice when they live this far north. But Southerners can't get enough ice in their drinks. My mom, a true Southerner, always orders her Diet Cokes the same way: with a lot (and I mean *a lot*— she'll send it back if you skimp) of ice.

After a decade in the South, I developed a habit of drinking a cold Diet Dr Pepper every morning. I knew the day would be hot, so I didn't want hot coffee to start it off. I also grew quite fond of ice-cold beer. Here in the North, I am clinging to these favorites for as long as I can. My new friends have an ongoing bet about how long it will be until I switch to hot coffee. They might soon win. It's true that holding a cold can of diet soda while walking the kids to school on a frosty 28-degree morning isn't ideal, so I am considering coffee. As for the other vice, my brother, Will, who lives and drinks cold beer in Holmes Beach, Fla., told me this: "You'd better switch to something that warms your belly—like Scotch."

Some things, however, don't change, no matter where you live. Just the other day, one of our neighbors brought home a freshly hunted deer. "He just strung that thing up by its feet," my son said flatly to my back as I washed dishes. He had seen plenty of hunters in Florida. Then my son said, "He left the deer hanging from a tree in his backyard."

I turned around, soap dripping from my hands. Oh, the stink that thing will cause, I thought. There will be flies everywhere! But the next day, on our walk to school, there wasn't even the slightest whiff of dead animal. There were no flies. And that's when it hit me. It's cold enough here in Maine to hang meat and keep it fresh. Until it freezes.

There Might Not Be Moose

For three years, I have disappointed Mainers and non-Mainers alike. When you live in a place like Maine, especially northern Maine, people want to know: Have you seen a moose? Have you seen Stephen King? And not necessarily in that order.

Until last week, I had not seen either.

I was beginning to think that both were a creation of the Maine Tourism Department. Unlike our former home state, Florida, where alligators (the mascot, if you will) are as plentiful as the Love Bugs in September, northern Maine's attractions are elusive and fabled to the point of frustration.

I finally conceded that Stephen King is indeed real after hearing too many accounts of people seeing him here and there. But the moose! Well, I had even convinced my children that there probably is no such thing, outside of the stuffed ones in every store at Bar Harbor.

Dustin said he saw a moose's rear end while he was riding a snowmobile in the western part of the state. Sure, I thought. A rear end. Could have been a horse or a deer.

I saw friends' moose antlers hanging like trophies on the walls of their basement, and I decided they were in on the scheme. Especially since one of those friends works for the state.

That same friend called me one day to tell me that a moose was on the loose in downtown Bangor. "Meet me at

Tri-City Pizza," he said, "and you will see it." A few minutes later, he called back. "Now the moose is in the Kenduskeag Stream. Oh, wait, now it's behind the post office."

Really?

When I finally caught up to our friend, the moose was supposedly "already gone."

Of course.

I dreamed about the day when I would finally see a moose, if, of course, they weren't an imaginary ploy. I dragged my family north and west in search of the animals. I always imagined that the one I saw would be about 10 feet tall, standing in a beam of light on the top of a boulder, like the father deer in *Bambi*. Or, I envisioned seeing one rising up from the surface of a lake, water pouring down its antlers.

I continued to hold out hope, even as my suspicions grew. It seemed a moose was always just behind or in front, but always eluding us. If we left Mount Katahdin at 3, someone saw a moose there at 3:10. If we were at Moosehead Lake on Sunday, someone had seen a moose there on Saturday.

Once, I overheard my son telling a friend, "Moose aren't real. They are just an advertising strategy for the state."

I saw these huge yellow warning signs on the side of the road: Caution, Moose Crossing. For the first two years, I slowed down and my heart beat faster. I didn't want to run into a moose on a dark highway. Our Realtor had told us that is how people die in Maine. And to post a caution sign, well, there must be hundreds of moose sightings in that area. Right? By the third year, I laughed at the warnings: "Sure, a 'moose crossing.' And I suppose pigs fly overhead, too."

Dustin grew so weary of my fruitless searches, sometimes he drove me long distances just to see a sculpture of a moose. This only confirmed my belief—er disbelief.

And then, last week, after taking my brother and his family to Pat's Pizza in Orono, we were driving down I-95 South when I spotted what looked like a horse on the side of the road.

"What is that?" someone in the back asked.

"I think it's . . . I think it's . . . oh my gosh, it's a moose!"

But it was a young moose with no antlers. It was sort of galloping alongside our car, and then it turned and went into the woods.

The car was quiet. Everyone held their breath, waiting for my reaction. Would I scream? Swerve off the road? Stop and take pictures?

I shook my head. "It didn't have antlers," I said. "I don't think I can count it if it isn't 10-feet tall, with antlers and water pouring off of them."

Dustin sighed.

Maybe I had built it up too much in my head. Like a prom or a wedding, the reality could never compare. Or maybe I really will be excited when I see a big one. In either case, Lindell, 4, cried in his car seat the rest of the way home. "It doesn't count unless it has antlers," he said. "Moose aren't real! They are fake."

I secretly agreed, even as I tried to calm down my son.

I suppose the state of Maine has us right where they want us.

STILL LOOKING FOR MOOSE

WHEN I TELL PEOPLE I LIVE IN MAINE, THEY ALMOST AL-
ways ask about the moose. Turns out, there are many misconceptions about moose, one being the idea that they out-
number people in Maine. The biggest misconception of all,
however, is probably that they exist to begin with.

The only moose I've seen is on the state flag.

Oh, all right, I supposedly saw an adolescent moose
running down I-95, but I'm not 100 percent sure that wasn't
a small horse. I didn't see antlers. And until I see a big bull
moose with 50-pound antlers, I won't be convinced the
species wasn't invented by the Office of Tourism to attract
tourists.

I've been on a mission to see a moose since I moved to
Maine in 2008. Previously, I was one of those never-been-
to-Maine types (I'm not a Mainer, but I got here as soon as
I could) who thought people in Maine probably kept the animals as pets or something. As I drove into the state for the
first time, the big moose-warning signs made me excited. I
was going to see one before I even had a house! Our Realtor
told me to be careful on the drive, because that's how people
die in Maine—they hit a moose. I thought I'd be dodging
them, for heaven's sake.

I never saw one. But taking all the best parts of what
Mainers had told me about the animals, I developed quite
the mental picture. I imagined them stepping over cars, com-

pletely unafraid of the highway, their legs like stilts casually moving in and out of traffic. People had told me moose eyes don't reflect light at night, so I wondered if maybe I had missed them altogether. Maybe they are that stealthy.

I knew friends who had seen moose. I saw their pictures on Facebook, and I studied them for indications that they'd been Photoshopped.

"You need to go further north," a friend who is a game warden told me. "Moose are everywhere up there. You're guaranteed to see one."

So last September I took the kids to Mount Katahdin, and I asked the rangers for the best spot to see moose.

"Definitely Sandy Stream," they said.

Down the path we went, rain jackets hanging from our arms just in case. When we got to the lookout at Sandy Stream, a couple was sitting there positively radiant from having just seen a moose, which, of course, was gone now.

"Also, last week I was here," the man said, "and, I'm not kidding, there were a dozen moose in the stream."

The boys and I sat at the lookout for as long as my youngest son, Lindell, could tolerate. We never saw anything.

Occasionally, throughout the year, my game warden friend would tell me about moose found wandering the city streets. I even put on the police scanner once and tried to follow the clues to a supposed moose bathing in the Kenduskeag Stream. By the time I got there, the moose was gone.

"Try going in the heat of the summer," my friend said. "They are more likely to be at the stream to cool off."

So last month, Dustin and I took the kids back up to Sandy Stream at Mount Katahdin. This time, we saw moose tracks along the trail. They were as big as Lindell's head, and I took about 20 photographs of them. I just knew I was about to see a moose this time. One of the kids stepped in moose poop—it went all the way up his shins and into his sock—and I could hardly stand the excitement. Who steps in moose droppings and doesn't actually see the animal?

Two professional photographers were on the lookout. They told us about all the moose they had seen "just yesterday."

"Everyone sees moose 'yesterday,'" my oldest son, Ford, said.

But there were no moose—none—in the stream that day. The park rangers had radioed their crews in the woods and instructed them to pull back the Office of Tourism-sponsored, mechanical, radio-controlled beasts because the Smileys were coming. (That's what they do, right?)

Or maybe I'm moose repellant.

A week later, I was on a bus in Washington, D.C., melting from the heat. The driver asked where I was from. When I told him Maine, I hoped he would ask me about lobster, Acadia National Park, loons or the snow. But I could tell by his face in the rearview mirror what he wanted to ask. He turned around in his chair and said, "Man, you must see a ton of moose up there! Do they, like, walk around in your backyard and stuff?"

He Who Hesitates Gets Stuck on the Lift

My oldest son, Ford, 9, has always been a sporty kid, but he isn't very fast. Dustin swears Ford has the unusual talent for running in slow motion. Ford is slow in all endeavors, from putting on his shoes to running to first base to retelling a story, especially when retelling a story.

Yet he has a positive attitude and a game-show-host smile that rivals most motivational speakers. These traits were never more apparent than when we took Ford skiing for the first time.

It was a beautiful day with plenty of sunshine and snow on the ground at Sugarloaf. Dustin and I looked forward to teaching our three boys how to ski. Of course, we hadn't accounted for the fact that corralling children, something like herding cats, while wearing heavy plastic ski boots would be difficult. But, whatever. We laughed at ourselves running with big, exaggerated steps, like walking on the moon, to chase Lindell, 3, around the rental equipment office. By the time we had suited up ourselves and the boys, we both were sweating.

Outside, we breathed in the fresh mountain air. The five of us stood in a row, our skis dug like walking sticks into the snow beside us, and admired the mountain. The skiers in the distance looked like a busy colony of ants working their way up and down a mound of sugar.

This is skiing, we told the boys. We paid no attention to the fact that we looked like a family from Florida who is more accustomed to watching the annual mullet toss on the Florida-Alabama state line than to understanding how and where to attach their lift tickets on their jackets.

Oh wait, we are that family from Florida.

We set down the five sets of skis and instructed the children to step their boots into the clips. This is when all heck broke loose. Owen, 7, and Lindell had a strong reaction, shall we say, to their child-size skis. I think Lindell's exact words were, "Get these things off of me. Get these things off of me right now." He looked like a crazy person.

While Dustin and I struggled to remove Owen's and Lindell's skis, our backs were turned to Ford, so we didn't realize, until it was too late, that Ford had already started down the beginner slope. Think Clark Griswold when he goes down the hill on a greased-up sled.

When I turned around to look, Ford was screaming "Whoa" and shooting down the mountain like a bullet. Other skiers were frantically looking over their shoulders and diving out of the way.

Dustin quickly stepped into his skis and went after Ford. He caught up to him near a makeshift ski jump. "Don't go over the jump," Dustin yelled to Ford. But it was too late.

Ford skied up the front of the jump and was propelled through the air off the back of it. This should have been enough to make any 9-year-old terrified and afraid of skiing. True to Ford's character, however, he came back up the hill, where I was still wrestling with Owen's and Lindell's skis. He was grinning ear to ear. I knew that Ford thought he was the best skier ever to go down the beginner slope at Sugarloaf.

Next it was my turn to ski with Ford. I love everything about skiing except the chairlift. Still, I put on a brave face for my son as the basket seat scooped us up, and we began a steady climb up the mountain. About halfway, I began my usual freakout session about how and when to get off the lift. "Relax, Mom," Ford said. He had all the confidence of a pro skier. So when I finally skied out of the chair and down the small hill at the lift's exit, I thought Ford would be right behind me.

"Whew, we made it," I said. "That's my least favorite part."

Ford didn't answer. I looked behind me. He was still on the chairlift and headed the other direction, back down the hill. He was screaming. "Whoa! Whoa!" Then, when the chair was about 2-3 feet above the snow, Ford jumped out. The lift came to a halt.

Fifteen minutes later, the lift was still not moving as technicians tried to fix whatever emergency stops my son had tripped. But Ford was already skiing down the hill again, oblivious to the commotion he had caused. He sped past skiers who had stopped on the slope to look up at the suspended chairlift. "Wonder who broke it," some of them said. Meanwhile, just past them, Ford was flying off the ski jump and screaming "Whoaaaa! Whoa!"

It was the fastest I had ever seen him move.

ICE FISHING

MOVING AROUND WITH THE MILITARY AFFORDS PEOPLE the opportunity to experience different cultures throughout our country and world. Because of this, and despite what some people believe, military families are usually the least sheltered or inexperienced.

Part of this education for military families involves area-specific activities, lingo and culture that can't (or won't) always be re-created in other places. In San Diego, for example, Dustin and I learned that the traffic on major roads is so reviled and legendary that instead of calling highways by their proper name ("Highway 5"), people insert an ominous, personified "The": "THE 5."

In Florida we learned about screen enclosures for pools and how they are the first thing to blow into your neighbor's yard during a hurricane. And when we lived along the Gulf of Mexico, just a stone's throw away from lower Alabama, we learned how to discern the good bull riders from the bad ones.

Last week, at our new duty station in Bangor, Dustin and I received an education in a totally new activity: ice fishing. (Did I mention that for all the things we have experienced during our travels, Dustin and I haven't always been the most talented when we participate in them?)

Our ice-fishing guide-teacher was our new friend Phil. Phil grew up around snow and ice. He plays ice hockey. He does ultimate fighting. Phil would never, ever fall—without throwing a few good punches first. You don't want to mess with Phil. Fish probably call him "The Phil."

My first clue that Dustin and I were totally out of our comfort zone should have been when we arrived at our friend's house and everyone there, except for us, was dressed in snow gear. With our jeans and water shoes, Dustin and I looked like we would be hunting for catfish.

My second clue was when we arrived at the "pond," which was more like a good-sized lake with ice as far as my eyes could see. I wanted to know where the wooden dock that I'd sit on was located. I might have asked, but then I noticed that Phil was already a half-mile ahead of us, walking effortlessly on the ice and carrying all the gear you need for ice fishing. (Hint: You don't cast out a hook and bait from a pole while you sit in a boat with warm water lapping at the sides.)

I imagine the next scene from Phil's perspective. When he looked over his shoulder to see if we were catching up and instead saw me, Dustin and the kids slipping and sliding on the ice like marbles rolling around a metal baking pan, he must have had second thoughts about bringing us.

I started this column saying that military families are not sheltered. Perhaps you think I was exaggerating now. I wasn't. I have bungee jumped four times, delivered three children, driven across country twice (once when I was almost eight-months pregnant), but when I stood on the edge of that frozen pond, about to take my first step and having only the hope that the water was as frozen as Phil said it was, I was scared. So was my son Owen.

"Owen's scared," I said to the group. "So I'll just stay here on the shore with him."

But Dustin wouldn't let me back out. He picked up Owen and we began our journey across the ice. Once the shore was very much out of reach, Dustin took one overly eager step, his feet came out from under him, and he landed, flat on his back. When he stood up, vanilla pudding was splattered all across the ice and Dustin's jacket.

Vanilla pudding? You're thinking: Why did they have vanilla pudding with them?

Phil was probably asking himself the same thing. We Smileys, of course, had packed a lunch with everything (minus the picnic blanket and basket) we thought we'd need for a day of "fishing." Now our lunch was all over the ice. And Dustin's jacket.

About an hour later, after I had finally arrived at an ice fishing hole and seen what it is about (Spoiler: You'll see more ice than fish or water—that's a good thing—when you go ice fishing), it was time to go home. Phil drove a pickup truck across the ice to get us. For me, that truck was like a raft floating in the water when you are drowning. If only I could get to the truck, my feet would have grip again.

Yet, at the truck's tailgate, my feet took one last slip, flew out from under me, and I landed backward on the ice, nearly sliding beneath Phil's legs.

Dustin still had pudding on his jacket.

Proving once again that you can take the Smileys around the country and the world, but if you want to look cool, you really can't take us anywhere.

OLD MAN WINTER

WHEN I FIRST ARRIVED IN MAINE IN AUGUST, IT WAS HARD to imagine this state as anything but sunny, pleasantly warm and full of lush greenery, shady trees and colorful flowers.

"Oh, but just you wait," my neighbors said. "Winter will come." They always said this with a playful smile, like I was about to sit on a whoopie cushion or something.

But never mind that, I thought. After spending a decade in Florida—where the ground is so parched you can imagine your front lawn actually catching fire from the sun, and blooms shrivel up and die horrible, crusty deaths—I was in awe at the mild climate of my new home.

By October, the shady green trees had turned vibrant variations of red, orange and yellow. Fallen leaves looked like little drops of sunlight on the concrete. The vision was so lovely, I nearly had a fender-bender driving my boys to school one morning because I couldn't stop staring at the trees.

By November, the boys had finally accepted the fact that there are no fire ants or snakes in our backyard. They spent hours wrestling in the fallen leaves, enjoying this newfound thing called "autumn."

"They won't be playing outside much longer," people said, with that same playful smile.

"Just wait until the trees are bare," my friend Bill said. "There's no turning back then."

In December, the days grew shorter, the wind got colder, and I felt a creeping sense of doom. I watched neighbors put out stakes to outline the perimeter of their driveways and yards.

"Strange," I thought. "Are they getting ready for a parade or something?"

I noticed people covering their bushes with wooden tents. My friend Tony's woodpile grew so tall, I could hardly see past it to his garage.

In my mind, Old Man Winter had become this ominous ogre looming on the outskirts of the city, waiting to strike. I had no idea what to expect. And judging by my neighbors' preparations, I knew that I wasn't ready, either.

Yet, I noticed that friends and neighbors did not make their preparations with any visible resentment or anger. In fact, they seemed to have an adrenaline-fueled eagerness. It would be another round of Man vs. Winter.

This healthy balance of respect mixed with fear is not unlike that of Floridians waiting for hurricane season. Winter storms and hurricanes have been around longer than we have. We are merely trying to make a go at it in their territory. But Floridians can go years, even decades, without a major storm. Mainers go up against their rival every year, like clockwork, once the trees are bare. Just like Bill said.

Except, it isn't entirely fair to call winter a "rival." Because, again, I sense that Mainers have a respect for the climate, even if it is sometimes a love-hate relationship. When Dustin and I venture outside after a storm to clear the driveway and sidewalk, passers-by and neighbors usually greet us with that playful smile again. It's as if we are all saying, "Well, winter might have won that round, but we'll try again next time." Their smile is not resigned. It's competitive, but jovial.

You see this same kind of good-spiritedness at the hill that kids use for sledding. As people struggle to climb the slippery slope with their sleds and tubes in tow, you get the idea that winter is somewhere off in the distance chuckling. But we're hanging in there, making the most of all the white stuff piled up like marshmallow Fluff. We may have leaks in our roofs, ice dams in our gutters and melted snow in the basement, but by golly, we're still standing for another round with Old Man Winter. Like a boxer who is bloodied and bruised, we come to the sledding hill and try to conquer the elements again with our cheap plastic sleds. Meanwhile, Old Man Winter is back in his corner, getting toweled off and saving his energy for the next round.

Every day on my way home from doing errands, I pass a cemetery. At the stop light beside it, I look over at what I can see of the graves and marvel at the thick blanket of snow on top of them. The people buried there spent their whole lives battling the snow. They shoveled it, raked it off the roofs, brushed it off their cars, cleaned it off their floors. In fact, many of them probably died with a snow shovel in hand. And now, there they lie, their last resting place clobbered with snow.

For a moment I feel sad. I am temporarily filled with the urge to go shovel the snow off all of the graves. Then I realize the Mainers lying there know Old Man Winter far better than I do. They have battled him many times, and now he has gently blanketed them with snow, like a football player patting a rival's back after a game.

The Mainers, I suspect, wouldn't have it any other way.

CRISPY ISN'T SPELLED WITH A K

FROM THE WAY MY SOUTHERN GRANDMOTHER HAS ALWAYS talked, I thought men in blue uniforms with rifles would be waiting for me when I crossed the Mason-Dixon Line on my way to Maine. It turns out, however, that the Mason-Dixon Line is not a line at all. I looked.

The only thing bearing any resemblance to a Mason-Dixon Line was the toll booths housing people who wanted my life savings. In the North, you pay for everything, including the privilege to drive on public roads that have very few exits.

In the South, blue reflective signs as big as small outhouses adorn the sides of highway to help drivers know which exits have a Waffle House and which ones don't (answer: not many). You can also find Krispy Kreme, Piggly Wiggly and Whataburger this way.

Not only does the North not have these exit signs, they don't use "Ks" for "Cs," either.

But never mind for a moment which stores and restaurants the North does or does not have. Once you get on the many turnpikes north of Maryland, you may never get off. We have something similar to this—something you enter and can't get back out, all while continuously emptying your wallet for reasons you're not sure of—in the South. We call them "casinos."

Driving north to our new home in Maine, I got on a turnpike in New Jersey, shortly before Owen, 5, announced his urgent need to find a bathroom, and many miles later, I was in New York, still on the turnpike, still unable to find an exit.

This is right around the time that I was introduced to the concept of "speeding traffic." In the South, traffic means that your car doesn't move. In New York, "traffic" often means that hundreds of cars, all within a few inches of one another, travel not slower, but faster than the speed limit. And no one cares that you didn't realize the exit you were looking for is on the left, not the right, until you are a quarter of a mile in front of it. Smiling out the window with a gosh-I-didn't-even-know expression doesn't help. In fact, I suspected that my Florida license plates were hurting my chances of getting across the 100-lane turnpike.

My grandmother has always, however unintentionally, made me think that northerners would be unfriendly. "Aloof" was a word I learned and associated with the North early in life. Yet on that road going through New York City, I learned otherwise. New Yorkers are definitely glad to speak to you, even if it means yelling through their closed car windows and making gestures with their fingers.

Then we entered Maine. It was as if we had crossed from one room in a house to another, and someone had just shut off all the lights in front of us. The smog and city lights of New York were far behind us, and even though we were still technically on a turnpike, there was only one other car in my rearview mirror. Okay, so it was 1 o'clock in the morning, but still. The world literally seemed to slow back down. Giant fir trees flanked the sides of the road, and the stars shone down like tiny pinpricks in the black sky.

At a gas station near Brunswick, I stopped to get a drink. I was 33 cents short.

"Ah, don't worry about it," the clerk said. "It's on me."

"For real?" I said, still digging through my purse.

"What's 33 cents?" she laughed. "Go on now. Get on the road."

Farther down the turnpike, I came to the last toll booth I would pass through before getting to Bangor.

"How much farther to Bangor?" I asked the attendant.

"About 88 miles," he said.

I took my change and got ready to drive off again. But the man stopped me.

"You going to be alright, miss?" he said.

I smiled and thanked him for caring.

"Yes," I said. "I think I'm going to be just fine."

The Beast Below the Floorboards

Moving from the deep South to the extreme North has afforded our family many new experiences. Some of these experiences—ones like seeing fallen autumn leaves that are so bright they look like drops of sunshine on the concrete—I eagerly endorse. Other experiences—such as putting two children who have never even roller-skated, much less ice-skated, on the ice for the first time at hockey practice—I strongly discourage. Nevertheless, I'd like to share some of the more memorable lessons from our first three months in Maine.

I'll begin with the furnace.

My husband, Dustin, was not here the first 2-and-a-half months I lived in Maine. He was finishing his tour in Pensacola, Fla., where he was working as a Navy flight instructor, and I came to our new duty station early to get the kids settled in school. Luckily, the temperatures in August and September did not call for learning about heating oil and furnaces on my own. There were many times, in fact, that I was hot. But my kids had a much harder time adjusting. Owen, whose life force is PediaSure and Goldfish crackers and therefore has very little body fat, suffered the most. By mid-September, Owen was wearing a ski hat and gloves to bed at night. But turning on the heater so soon, when most Mainers were still wearing flip-flops, seemed ridiculous.

Well, okay, the truth is, I was afraid to turn on the furnace. I have never had a basement before, so I didn't know what a furnace and the underbelly of vents, pinned to the ceiling like giant, steel spaghetti, really looks like. And I've never had an oil tank, either. Every time I ventured into the basement to fetch a load of laundry, I made a deal with the oil tank-furnace duo: "You stay in your corner and I'll stay in mine. No one gets hurt."

The oil tank, a big barrel of a thing that looks like something people in my hometown in Virginia use to cook pigs, seemed very ominous. "You mean it's full of oil, right there in my basement?" I asked a new friend. "Is that safe?"

But the furnace . . . Oh, the furnace! The furnace scared me the most. It was like a dragon coiled up in the middle of the basement, and I had no desire to wake the beast. Then, in October, the temperatures started to dip more. Even the Mainers were putting on coats. It was time to turn on the furnace. And Dustin still wasn't home.

The first time I set the thermostat and the dragon woke up, it hissed and clanked and grumbled. An awful smell—dust mixed with mildew and . . . gas?—rose up from the floor vents. The wooden floorboards seemed to vibrate. I shut off the furnace and told the boys to put on another layer of clothes.

But it was getting cold at night.

I had a talk with the dragon, I mean, furnace: "Look, you stay in your neck of the woods, and I'll stay in mine. Just give us some heat. And try not to be so angry, would you?"

One month later, I've made peace with the furnace and all of its racket. I've even grown quite fond of it. Jet noise may be the sound of freedom, but furnace-clanking is the sound of warmth. I even fixed a broken vent all by myself.

No, I'm not afraid of the beast in the basement anymore. In fact, I hardly notice it anymore.

And then I got our first bill.

My Basement of Solitude

Growing up, I always lived "below sea level" (at least that is what my parents said, which made me feel like a fish) and therefore never had a basement. Try to dig for a basement in my hometown of Virginia Beach, Va., and you'll end up with a pool.

My only experience with basements was my grandparents' in Birmingham, Ala. That's where my older brothers often lured me with hopes of including me in their play ("Come down in the basement with us, Sarah, and we'll play Chutes and Ladders with you"), only to run back upstairs and lock the door, leaving me in the dark room alone. My grandparents had a life-size wooden Santa Claus in the back corner, rising above trunks of old clothes and photo albums, and sometimes I was sure I saw his upraised hand wave at me.

In any case, the junk in my grandparents' basement, most of which belonged to my grandfather, led me to believe that the whole idea of a room under the earth was a man's idea. I mean really, would a woman ever think of this? The men already monopolize garages with their tools and ugly posters that we won't let them hang in the house; why not expand to the basement, too?

When Dustin and I lived in Florida, our garage was his domain. Not coincidentally, the garage was always a mess. Theoretically, it was a "two-car garage," but fitting two cars in there side-by-side only worked if we pushed in the side mirrors and climbed out the back hatch.

One time I found a dead mouse in our garage and was so scared I convinced Dustin to put out sticky boards to catch the mouse's friends and family. The next day, one of those sticky boards caught a coral snake which, no doubt, also smelled the dead mouse and planned to eat it. This event, plus Dustin's tendency to rescue items from our garage sales and stack them in a large heap in the corner of the garage, heralded my decision to never use the garage. Not ever. It became the official place for storing Dustin's old sea bags, undershirts and socks turned gray from six-month deployments on an aircraft carrier, and all the tacky things that Dustin would not let me sell at a garage sale.

Then we moved to Maine, where almost everyone has a basement. "Great," I thought, "the basement will be my area and Dustin can have the garage." Before we closed on our new house and moved in, I daydreamed about making the unfinished basement a guest room or a playroom for the boys.

"What? I'm not coming to visit if I have to sleep in an unfinished basement that isn't heated," my mom said.

"We have to play in the basement?" the boys asked. "Isn't that kind of like playing in the garage or something?"

None of us had a clue what owning a basement would really be like. Turns out, basements are pretty cool. Literally. We moved into our house in mid-August, and although the weather was considerably cooler than in our previous home state of Florida, I did work up a sweat unloading boxes and moving furniture. Sometimes, the only way I could cool down (because our house doesn't have air-conditioning, something that would make my Florida friends choke on their own breath) was to go down into the basement and sit on the cool concrete floor.

I still planned to make the basement a playroom, but then, I had not accounted for the fact that my boys were terrified of it. Meanwhile, I maintained my preference for avoiding the garage at all costs, which turns out to be a foolish idea because a car left out in the cold in New England tends to freeze and not cooperate in the morning.

But the basement, well, it has become my hideaway—my escape. Because the boys are still afraid of it, the basement is the only place in our house where I can go uninterrupted. Even my own bathroom can't offer the same solitude. Sometimes I pretend to do laundry down there, when really I'm just sitting. Yep, just sitting—without anyone whining, tattling or wiping their runny nose on the furniture beside me.

And for this reason alone, I have come to understand that my initial thoughts about basements were wrong. A room beneath the house couldn't have been a man's idea. It must have been a mother's.

Benefits of Small Living

Dustin and I had a large house in Florida. Most people there do. Perhaps it is the heat, which even in the middle of October still can feel as hot as the air from a hair dryer (only with less wind), but most homes in Florida are sprawling. Two-story houses are an anomaly; the bigger the footprint of a house in Florida, the better. This makes it so that no one ever has to touch or be near anyone else in their family. And in that type of heat, who would want to?

Our house was also typical in that it was covered almost entirely with tile floors. Carpet gets too sticky when you're hot. And just like the majority of children nearby, our boys had a large playroom and separate bedroom. They had their own bathroom, too, which I am told stayed remarkably clean most of the time, but I can neither confirm nor deny this because unless I had a reason to venture into the boys' bathroom, I didn't see it. That's how big our house was. We had two extra bedrooms and one extra bathroom that were furnished but ultimately not used. We could have stored a minivan in our attic.

So you can imagine our surprise when we were moving to Maine, and an online search revealed that very few homes are larger than 2,000 square feet. I fell in love with one that is just barely 1,500 square feet.

"The house is perfect, but it just seems, I don't know, kind of small," I said to our real estate agent.

"You've never had to pay a heating bill, have you?" he said.

On moving day, our boys shamelessly cried when we gave away almost three-quarters of the toys that once filled their playroom in Florida. There just wasn't any room for them. It was my turn to pout, however, when we had to store my piano and the dining room set my grandmother gave to me. I was beginning to believe that our rented storage unit was roomier than our new house.

But then an interesting thing happened. While I swept the kitchen floor, I could hear my boys through the wall, playing in their bedroom, talking to each other about the scariest dream they had ever had, their favorite new friends, and their best and worst subjects in school.

Had they always talked with each other like this?

Whereas they used to go up to their playroom to watch movies and cartoons, now they had to share the living room with everyone else. As I typed on my computer in the kitchen, I could hear the dialogue of the television program and intervene when necessary.

Was *The Clone Wars* always this violent? And when had the boys stopped watching *Franklin*? What other conversations and insights had I missed when my children were upstairs, shut in their playroom?

Once I was in the basement folding laundry when I heard Ford and Owen teasing their little brother, Lindell. I directed my mouth at the ceiling and yelled, "Cut it out or you're both grounded," and like a snake sneaking up on its prey and bouncing forward to strike, my voice came through the vents on the floor into the boys' bedroom. They were stunned into silence. Maybe Mom does have eyes in the back of her head, I imagined them thinking.

One year later, I can't imagine living in a large house. Much like soldiers in barracks or college students in dormitories, my family is bonding. We are under each other's foot, in each other's business, but finally living with each other, if not on top of each other. Before, I wasn't sure how my boys would handle sharing a small room and not having a playroom. "I never had my own room until I joined the Navy," my dad said. "And I never had a playroom." He turned out just fine. Maybe even better because of it.

In hindsight, our old house was excessive. Our voices echoed off the tall ceilings and wide, open living room, signifying to me the distance that had grown between my family. Our voices don't echo anymore. They seep through the floorboards, out the open screen windows (maybe our neighbors know us a little too well), and through the vents in the next room.

One day, as I was getting dressed upstairs, I heard my boys talking in their room below. "Remember how Mom seemed kind of sad before?" Ford said.

"Yeah, she's much happier now," Owen said.

I smiled to myself, my heart full and grateful. Then I put my lips to the vent on the floor and whispered, "I love you guys."

Silence.

No Room for Lazy

My family was unprepared for our first winter in Maine. We didn't even put away our patio furniture or place wooden teepees over our bushes. I remember watching a neighbor rake his roof one cold morning while Dustin and I were still in our pajamas. Dustin stood at the window with his coffee. "Our neighbor must really like a clean roof," Dustin said. We both laughed. Then we went back to the family room to watch television.

A few weeks later, we learned (the hard way) about ice dams.

Resting is not an option in Maine. You have to work (i.e., shovel the sidewalk and plow the driveway) before you can even get out the door to go to work. I'm sure it qualifies as aerobic activity to put three children in mittens, hats and snow boots, AND get them to school on time. Even throwing out your trash isn't as simple as hurling the bag over your shoulder and stuffing it into the garbage can. If the lid is frozen, you have to chip away at the ice first. I couldn't get into my car last year without blowing hot air on the keyhole (followed by stomping my feet and kicking the tires when the door was still frozen shut and the kids were 10 minutes late for school).

Mainers are accustomed to this kind of life. Being "from away," I once felt sorry about the gravestones at Mount Hope Cemetery that have been clobbered with snow. People spend their whole lives shoveling the snow, wiping it from their windshield, and raking it off their roof. Then, at the end, they are buried in it. One Maine winter later, however, I know that graves covered with snow—the last round with Old Man Winter—might be considered a badge of honor for Mainers, who even in death don't expect the easy way out.

This is 180 degrees from the attitude of Floridians, where, aside from the occasional hurricane and rogue snake, life is pretty darn easy. In Florida, not only do most people have a pool, they also have large screen enclosures (the first thing to blow away in a hurricane, by the way) built around them to keep the bugs and most of the heat and sun out. Entire neighborhoods are developed around golf courses. (When we lived on the 17th hole of one such course, I saw golfers who were too hot to push their own carts, so they used remote controls.)

And the beach is at the center of everyone's life. You don't winterize your house or lawn in Florida, and the only time you go onto your roof is to jump from it into the pool (not recommended).

I see now that Florida—and in particular, beach towns—can effortlessly (pun intended) breed laziness. There is no rush. No deadline. No sense of battling the elements on a regular basis. (Granted, some Florida roaches can be killed only with the most aggressive Ultimate Fighting techniques, and maybe a shotgun, but still.)

At first I was shocked by the amount of work required to live in Maine. Now I couldn't imagine raising my boys in any other environment. I mean, how can people know true relaxation if they've never had to shovel snow for two hours before going to work? How can you enjoy the warmth if you've never felt the chill? I don't think it's possible, and that's why, if given the choice between Florida and Maine, I will always choose the latter.

The GPS Won't Get You to Katahdin

Despite having a GPS in our car and on my iPhone, Dustin and I still manage to get lost.

Basically, there are two types of people when it comes to GPS. There are those who distrust the machine at every turn: "It says, 'Turn left on State Street,' and I see State Street on my left, but I'm not sure. I think I'll go up a few blocks and find a different State Street." Then there are those who will follow the GPS like the Holy Grail through a bamboo forest, if that's what the device suggests, just to get to the grocery store: "The GPS says, 'Turn left on State Street,' and all I see is a curb and an office building, but what the heck, I think I'll turn left."

Dustin is the first kind of person. I am like the second. This makes for interesting car trips.

GPS (always spoken with a British accent because that's the way Owen likes it): "In 400 yards, turn right, and then turn left."

Dustin: "Why would it tell us to turn right and then left? I think I'll go left and then turn right instead."

Me: "I think we should do what the GPS tells us to do."

Dustin: "But there's a lake to our right, Sarah."

Me: "Well, maybe it knows something we don't."

There are many times when I am sure the next words out of our GPS guide will be, "I think the 3-year-old who just wet his trousers in the back seat could drive better than you nitwits."

Yet we have seen many parts of the country we otherwise might never have without our unique relationships with the GPS. I grew up near Norfolk, Va., and for the 20 or so years I lived there, I never drove through some of the seedier inner-city neighborhoods. However, because I will follow my GPS to the ends of the Earth, two years ago I found myself rolling through Norfolk's most notorious street in my mom's shiny Ford Edge. The people on the curb—most of them teenagers with their pants hanging down—smirked, and it occurred to me that since the inception and widespread use of GPS, they must have grown used to seeing "outsiders" in their formerly, and legendarily, off-limits neighborhoods. I wondered whether they looked at my car and said, "Must be another GPS."

Last week, Dustin and I, together with my brother, Van, and sister-in-law, Kelly, who were visiting from Virginia, "explored" (code for we got lost) a new area around Mount Katahdin in northern Maine. Here was the problem: When the device asked for a destination, we gave it "Mount Katahdin." Now, Mount Katahdin is a very large mountain, and it isn't passable by car. But the GPS lady, God bless her British heart, did the best she could before we realized the mistake.

First we were driving up Interstate 95. All good so far. Next we exited at the town of Millinocket. Still good. Eventually we merged onto the famed Golden Road, where the local logging industry made its wealth. This is where the GPS lady did us wrong. We followed the Golden Road for many miles, deep into the woods of northern Maine, until the road became gravel and dirt. When the GPS said, "In one-half mile, turn right," we looked for a road that we hoped would be the entrance to Baxter State Park. Instead we found a barely cleared back-forest trail, and because I was in the driver's seat, we turned onto it anyway. The minivan snapped tree limbs and catapulted rocks as we bounced along the rugged pathway. Van and Kelly had hoped to see a moose, but I'm sure all the animal kingdom ran when they saw us coming: "Crikey! This one's coming through in a minivan!"

When we realized the GPS was trying to take us to the summit of Mount Katahdin, by way of circling the base first, we stopped to look at a good old paper map. We were on the other side of the mountain from Baxter State Park.

That night, when I turned on my computer, I saw the Web page that I last had visited the morning before our trek. It was the Baxter State Park "Directions" page. I scrolled down and found something I should have read 12 hours earlier:

"Commercial navigation units are not effective for navigating to the Park. Visitors have had unpleasant, time-consuming and expensive experiences using GPS units to navigate to the Park. Our headquarters address is 64 Balsam Drive, Millinocket, Maine 04462. Headquarters is 18 miles from the South Park Entrance at Togue Pond Gate and over 60 miles from the North Entrance at Matagamon Gate."

WHEN A CASE OF SODA FREEZES,
YOU KNOW IT'S COLD

SOMETHING I'VE NOT QUITE ADJUSTED TO HERE IN MAINE
is the unpopularity of ice. I'm not talking about the sheet
of ice on the sidewalk or the long stalactites hanging from
the eaves. That ice is met with half-hearted dislike by most
adults. The ice I'm talking about is the kind Southerners do
not go without, the kind that is piled high and deep at the
bottom of a glass of tea.

Perhaps Northerners are sick of winter and ice, so the
last place they want to find something cold is in a drinking
glass. Or maybe Northerners take ice for granted. Either
way, refrigerators with automatic ice dispensers on the
door—a sign of true luxury in the South—are hard to come
by up here. I have a friend in Bangor who drinks her soft
drinks warm, straight out of the pantry.

For someone like me, however, who drinks a Diet Dr
Pepper every morning (don't judge, coffee-drinkers—it's
caffeine) and likes it cold, the scarcity of ice for drinks is a
problem. In the South, my drink order was served like this:
ice with a little splash of soda. In the North, it's more like:
soda with a few pebbles of ice floating at the top.

You know my mom—born and raised in Birmingham,
Ala.—is visiting when you see bags of ice stocked in my
refrigerator. What won't fit inside sits on the back porch,
where for six months of the year it is actually colder than

the freezer. Mom always orders her drinks the same: "a large Diet Coke with a lot of ice." (If she can stir the liquid with her straw and the straw doesn't bend and snap against the ice, there isn't enough.) Here in Bangor, that amounts to: soda with a few (extra) pebbles floating at the top.

In time, I've learned to creatively manage this ice dilemma. For starters, my cans of Diet Dr Pepper are generally colder than normal straight out of the pantry due to the overall temperature in Maine. It doesn't take much to get them up to drinking standard. In a pinch, putting the can in the freezer for a good 10-15 minutes will work. However— and this is very important!—after about 20 minutes, the soda will freeze, the contents will expand, and the aluminum can will burst.

Actually, on second thought, "burst" doesn't adequately capture the violence with which the soda explodes. "Burst" suggests a breaking point, but it has happy connotations, such as "bursting with happiness" and "bursting with pride." To be sure, I'm bursting with something when I open the freezer and see brown slush spewed across every surface, but it isn't happiness or pride. What a frozen can of soda does inside a freezer is detonate. Sometimes you can even hear the pop when it happens. That's when you quickly run away and let your spouse be the first to open the door and see the mess (finders keepers!).

Speaking of my spouse, Dustin is just as guilty of leaving sodas in the freezer. Only he drinks diet root beer, not Dr Pepper. Therefore, the aftermath of an explosion is like a hot potato: No one wants to be left with the cleanup. But root beer and Dr Pepper are both brown. Often it is difficult to determine whose mess it is, especially when the guilty party quickly gets rid of the offending can but leaves the slush behind. You might think I'm above getting on my hands and knees and licking the floor, but you are wrong. If tasting the slush is what's required to accuse Dustin, I'm so not above that.

At Christmas, my dad had the great idea to leave cases of soda on the front porch to keep them cold and ready for the morning. The porch, which is not heated, was about 20 degrees. Instant freezer! This method worked beautifully until last week, when temperatures dipped well below zero (dangerously cold for carbonated beverages under pressure).

I remember hearing the pop. I was lying in bed, and I thought, "I wonder if a picture fell off the wall." But then I fell asleep.

The next morning, as the kids and I were putting on our snow boots, I saw brown slush, like a splatter of paint, on the wall behind me. I looked up, and then around. Similar splotches, some bigger than others, surrounded me. They were on the ceiling, the walls, the windows and the furniture. In fact, the porch looked like a (frozen) crime scene. And then I saw the ripped-apart cardboard box and one of my dad's sodas on the floor. The top had been blown clean off the can.

Previously I thought that a frozen soda detonating in the freezer was the worst thing ever. I was wrong. Twelve frozen sodas exploding on the front porch is much worse.

How to Blow Snow

FOR MILITARY SPOUSES, IT IS AN OMINOUS SIGN WHEN YOUR service member loved one suddenly says something like, "I need to teach you how to start the weed whacker." Or, "The car will need an oil change in about six months." This usually means he has a hunch he is leaving soon. It reminds me of when I was a kid and I saw my mom take frozen fish sticks and french fries out of the oven. That meant we were having a baby sitter.

It has been awhile since Dustin raised one of these subtle red flags. In fact, the last time I can recall was when he briefed me on hurricane preparation procedures ("move the patio furniture to the garage, fill the bathtub with water, and whatever you do, make sure my golf clubs are secure") just before Hurricane Ivan hit us in Pensacola, Fla. This was expected; when a natural disaster looms, Navy pilots flee to protect their taxpayer-funded aircraft. Dustin was having barbecue in Tennessee by the time Ivan chased me and the boys up a crowded northbound interstate.

It has been so long since then, however, I almost forgot how my stomach goes cold and my throat gets tight when Dustin drops one of these foreshadowing bombs. Until last week.

We were both outside doing our usual snow removal routine: Dustin rakes the roof and handles the snowblower while I shovel the walkway and back porch. I was content to be lost in my own mind, thinking of the week ahead, when suddenly the purr of the snowblower stopped, and I heard Dustin yell, "Wanna come over here so I can teach you how to start this thing?"

Um, no. That was my first thought. Then: Why do I need to know that when I have you here to start it for me?

An important note about our snowblower: It isn't ours. It has been graciously loaned to us by our elderly neighbor under the condition that we clear his driveway, too. The first time I saw Dustin use the snowblower, I laughed so hard I got warm and I had to shed winter layers. Tears of laughter froze on my cheeks. I sat down in a pile of snow and slapped my hand against my knee. Dustin was pushing against what seemed like an immovable mass of metal until his feet slipped out from under him. He kicked snowbanks and cursed at the wind.

Meanwhile, our neighbor Tony across the street was guiding his snowblower with one hand and waving to us with the other. Tall and muscular, Tony is an exaggerated inverted triangle. As he made effortless loops up and down his driveway, he looked like a man pushing a child's play stroller.

Dustin was still grunting at our snowblower and sweating through his wool hat.

When Tony had finished his driveway, he came over to ours and gave Dustin a lesson in Snowblowing 101. I was already inside getting warm. With Dustin home, there was no reason for me to know how to use the snowblower.

All that has changed now.

Dustin guided my hand to the metal lever that rumbled and vibrated. "Just push this forward when you want to move," Dustin yelled over the noise of the engine. "That will take the machine out of neutral."

I pushed the lever as he had instructed, and suddenly the snowblower lurched forward. It was an experience like walking an overly excited dog. I didn't guide the snowblower so much as it dragged me. I imagine this to be what walking an elephant would is like.

However, I quickly learned that the chute that spits out a stream of snow, the one that is controlled by a crank, is kid repellent. Our boys were running for their lives, diving this way and that, trying to avoid the steady blast of snow coming out of the snowblower. I reasoned that the chute also might be husband repellent. Then I remembered that I want Dustin in a good mood so that he will clear snow—and not ever leave me.

In about 20 minutes, I had cut a walkway from our front yard to our neighbor's driveway. I stood back to admire my work and consider the ramifications: Now that I had demonstrated proficiency with the snowblower, what would be my excuse?

Dustin came around the corner with the roof rake. He motioned for me to come over. I knew that he wanted to show me "just one more thing," to give me "another lesson."

This didn't look good.

I ran inside the house, put my fingers in my ears and pretended not to know what was happening, what all of this meant. Which is to say, I chose to believe my husband is not in the military. Turns out, Dustin will leave in October.

Later that day, I peeked out my window and saw Tony pushing his snowblower with one hand. He waved at a passer-by. I was suddenly calm knowing he would always be there. Dustin is, too. It's not unusual for Tony to dash into my house at times when he thinks the repairman's truck has stayed outside too long or when he saw black smoke coming out of the chimney. And besides teaching a spouse how to survive on her own, a military man like Dustin always makes sure there is a neighbor keeping watch when he cannot.

When I Knew Maine Was Home

Roof rakes for sale at the hardware store was one of the first new things I noticed when we moved to Bangor two years ago. I asked Dustin, "Why do you suppose someone would rake their roof?" He just shrugged.

Also, when I asked for directions, people usually answered with something like, "Go down to what used to be the old drugstore, then turn left at the Adams' old house, the one they sold last year. Go a block or so, and you'll know you're there when you're so close to the elementary school that you could throw a football into the playground and hit the seesaw."

A new friend I had just met suggested that we get the kids together for dinner. It was fall and the daylight was getting shorter.

"How about 6:30 at my house?" I said.

My new friend looked like she would choke. "You realize it will be dark by 3:45, right? How about a 5 o'clock supper?"

In Florida, we never ate before 6:30 p.m. Also, we didn't call it supper.

I fell in love with Maine during those first few months in 2008. Everything—from the way the heater smelled when it first kicked on to the boots people stepped out of on their front porch to the puddle of slush they left behind—was endearing. There wasn't a day that passed when I didn't learn something about my new hometown. And just like falling in love, I was keenly aware of Maine's every nuance.

I learned that the Corner Store on Hammond Street is more than just a place to buy bread, and I was sure to see someone I knew there. I learned that there isn't just one type of snow, but only one type that makes really good snowmen. In the summer, I learned that when all the windows are open and the neighbors are sitting on their front steps to catch a breeze, everyone can hear you yell at your kids.

Snowblowers firing up early in the morning after a storm, and snowplows passing by and scraping the pavement, were things that woke me from a sound sleep. ("What the heck was that?") The basement was a novelty—"You mean I can just ask the kids to go play in the basement when they are getting too loud upstairs?" (New friend: "Yes")—and the abundance of older homes was an endless source of fascination. No two houses have the same blueprint; I actually have to ask, "Where is your bathroom?"

As with all relationships, however, as the years passed, I grew to take things about Maine for granted. Acadia Mountain, while still awesome and spectacular, didn't take my breath away in quite the same way. Giant snowflakes were no longer cause to get out from under my blankets and rush to the window. I finally owned a roof rake and knew how and when to use it.

The process of falling in love was complete. I had become one with Maine (though still not a "Mainer," of course). I was no longer on the outside looking in. I was the person giving directions that included not one single mention of "north" or "south." I had been the person with wide eyes, shaking up a snow globe and watching the snowflakes fall. Then I was the person inside the globe, semi-unaware of the uniqueness of my surroundings.

I try to explain Maine and why I love it here to friends I left behind in other states. But it's becoming increasingly more difficult to separate what is particular to Maine and what is not. Because it all has become "home" to me.

This August, my older brother Van and his wife, Kelly, came to visit. Looking back, I should have noticed the way they stared out the window, taking in things that I now failed to see, as I drove through the city. But few aspects of life in Maine seemed unusual to me anymore.

Then Van said, "There's another one." He was pointing out the windshield.

"Another what?" I asked.

"Another house preparing for winter," he said. "I've never seen so many houses getting new roofs at the same time."

I looked out the windows, first to the left and then to the right. On either side of us, men squatted on roofs and threw down old shingles. Van was right, and it's another unique aspect of Maine: August is filled with the sound of hammers as roofers hurry to make repairs before winter. It seemed so natural to me now, as commonplace as drying mittens on the floor next to the heater or the sound of icicles falling from the eaves and crashing on the back porch.

That's when I realized that Maine had truly become my home. But I wonder, why did it take me so long to get here?

THE WAY LIFE IS

Waking the Senses

It was a warm April Fool's Day in Pensacola, Fla.—
the kind of day when a blanket of hissing bugs rises up from
the grass as you step in it—when I first heard the news that
our family was being transferred to Maine. I immediately
got online and searched message boards and forums to find
people who lived there.

"Is it really as cold as people say?" I asked.

"I have 6 feet of snow in my yard right now," someone
wrote back.

Our neighbor across the street, also a Navy pilot who
had just finished a tour in Brunswick, chuckled when I told
him about our new orders. He was washing his boat after a
day of fishing in the Gulf of Mexico. When he stopped to
reminisce about his time in Maine, he had that faraway look
in his eyes that people often get when they think back to
another time or expeditions in foreign countries, things that
only make sense if you've been there, too.

"Tell me what it's like," I said.

"Cold."

My anxiety rose. And yet, there was a part deep inside of
me, as yet unrecognized and inexplicable, that was ready for
the challenge. In fact, I yearned for it, and I didn't know just
how much until that moment.

If you've never lived in an area of the country where
the seasons change very little, you might be able to gain

an appreciation for the experience if you go down to your basement, wipe off the old treadmill and walk on it for about an hour. When you are finished, nothing will have changed. You will stand right where you began. And because you're in the basement, you may not even know if it has begun to rain or not. Left down there all day with no clock and not much daylight, you'd begin to have no idea if it was morning or night.

This is what living in a tropical climate sometimes feels like, minus the basement and the lack of sunshine, of course. If I woke from a coma in the middle of Florida, I would not be able to tell you, based on surroundings alone, what time of year it was. No, I take that back. If stores were decorated with cut-out Santa Clauses holding surfboards and wearing leis, I might know that it was December. But the other 11 months are anyone's guess.

After a decade in Florida, I began to feel like my senses were stunted. Colors were muted. Smells were flat and my ears were plugged. I didn't even hear the birds chirping any more. Why should I? They were always there. They had become part of the background noise, mixed with the sound of passing cars and children playing outside (because children can always play outside in Florida). The sky was always blue; the sun hot. And I failed to appreciate either delight anymore.

One day, when Owen, now 6, was about 2 years old, I read a book to him about kids making a pile of leaves and jumping in them. "Mommy, why would leaves fall off the trees?" he asked. I looked outside his bedroom window.

Although it was technically fall, pine trees stood like soldiers with the blazing sun beating down on their bark. The grass was as green as it was in June. That's when I realized that my son had been deprived of one of life's greatest treasures: the passing of seasons.

How can you appreciate a forest full of leafy green trees if they have been that way 365 days a year? How can you appreciate the sunshine when you've never gone without it? What does spring really mean if the flowers and plants have been blooming all along?

People thought my feelings about Maine would change after experiencing my first winter. And they did change—for the better.

Winters are hard, but without them, spring means very little. Waiting for spring after three months of snow feels like waiting for a good sneeze. Never have I longed so much for flowers and warmth. Already, I have come to understand that it is one of life's miracles to see the first green leaves of a hosta poking through the holes of melted snow. Each time I go outside, I'm like a child experiencing the world for the first time. I suspect my boys have grown tired of me pointing out each new bud on the trees, every squirrel digging up nuts in the front yard. Except, it's been hard getting the boys off their bicycles at dinnertime, and they wrestle in the newly uncovered backyard as if they've never seen it before. Maybe we all feel more awake.

I am reminded of Maine's own E.B. White reflecting on daily life at a saltwater farm in Maine in the foreword to his collection of essays *One Man's Meat*: "Once in everyone's life there is apt to be a period when he is fully awake, instead of half asleep. . . . I was suddenly seeing, feeling, and listening as a child sees, feels, and listens."

Lucky for those of us in Maine, this rebirth happens again and again, each year when the chill of winter gives way to the warmth of spring.

Off the Beaten Path in the County

Since the integration of GPS on our devices into our everyday life, I have found myself off the beaten path more often. That seems counterintuitive, doesn't it? With better navigation and a hands-free, robot voice giving step-by-step directions, I should be getting from Point A to Point B more directly. Except, it seems that iPhone's Siri, in particular, has a mind of her own, and I sometimes end up in unchartered territory when I follow her commands.

And I do follow her commands. Dustin does not. Dustin knows better than Siri. He tempts fate by seeing the exit she told him to take, and then passing it by because "it doesn't seem like the right one."

"Always follow Siri," I tell him. "It doesn't matter what you think. You don't know what Siri knows."

Sometimes Siri can predict traffic. Sometimes she knows about detours. She's like a wizard on the dashboard, and I do not second guess her. Even when I fear she's sending me off track.

This happened last week when I headed north for a book club event in Houlton, which, for anyone south of Houlton, basically feels like Canada. Indeed, Houlton is near the very top of the map, and as I drove, I had a distinct feeling of climbing a vertical wall, like my car was literally traveling up the United States and teetering on the top.

Interstate 95 is the main road to Houlton, and I'm no stranger to it. When we lived in Jacksonville, Fla., I used I-95 daily. There, it passes by the Jaguars' stadium and winds through high-rise buildings. When Dustin and I traveled from Jacksonville to our hometowns in Virginia, the directions basically were, "get on I-95, head north for 700 miles, and then get off I-95."

Since moving to Maine, we travel the northeastern part of I-95 on family vacations through Massachusetts, New York City, New Jersey and Washington, D.C. Despite minor differences, in all these areas, I-95 is basically the same. But the stretch of it that runs from Bangor to Houlton is so different that it almost deserves another name. Here, the road signs become sparse (except for the moose warnings, of course), and there are no billboards or rest stops. There are very few exits and long stretches of road where there is nothing but pine trees. Indeed, I had a Bill Murray moment from "What About Bob?" when I realized I was totally alone on I-95 for about 30 minutes on my way to Houlton last week.

Siri was unusually quiet. She had no instructions to give except, maybe, "keep going north . . . for a very long time."

But somewhere around Sherman, her voice pierced the silence. She wanted me to take the next exit, even though I was still about an hour away from the destination. I was skeptical and a little afraid. But remember, I always follow Siri.

I left I-95 in my rear view mirror and merged onto a long, winding road that seemed even more lonely than the one before. Now, I was terrified. What if I lost my signal and Siri left me stranded on a deserted road in northern Maine?

I held my breath as I drove, but soon, general stores and empty gas stations gave way to hillsides dotted with grand, old homes with attached barns. Cows grazed in the fields. There was no hustle and bustle here. No cars zooming past. No honking, billboards or stop lights. Just quiet. And sometimes it's hard to be quiet. I worried about my schedule—Would I be on time?—and the directions—Where was I?—and yet I kept following Siri.

Then I came around a bend and saw the most spectacular sight: behind the cows and the orange and red autumn leaves, Mt. Katahdin rose in the distance. Clouds hugged the top of the mountain, but sun shone all around the base. I stopped my car in the middle of the road, which didn't matter because there was no one else around. The tires landed on a pile of cow manure, and the earthy smell filled my nose as I rolled down the window to take a picture. The picture didn't do the vision justice. I moved on.

It's a good thing the world is slower and less crowded up there, because I was a reckless driver peering at the views and snapping pictures at every turn. I was sad when Siri told me to get back on I-95.

I don't know why the GPS sent me off the highway for 45 miles that day. There seemed to be no reason for it. On my way home, I tried to take the detour again, but Siri insisted I use I-95 instead. As I drove, I caught distance glimpses of the hillsides, cows and barns, and for a moment, I was insanely jealous of all those people over there, off the beaten path.

Small, Local Shops Make Memories

We had always lived in metropolitan areas, places where the prospect of a new Linens 'N Things–PetSmart–Barnes & Noble shopping center would elicit excitement comparable to that of children on Christmas morning. Residents actually lobbied to bring large, warehouse-style stores to the area. People delighted in another new fast-food restaurant because it made their lives easier and the city busier. Indeed, a new Ruby Tuesday or big-box pharmacy assured us that all was right in the world. Without them, what would become of the community?

I dragged my kids to these chain stores. We called it "doing errands," and the boys hated it. "Moooom, do we haaave to go?" they said. Once inside, they made their point by stuffing their growing legs and feet into the shopping cart and staring at their handheld video games. By the end, they had no idea whether they had been to PetSmart, Costco or Linens 'N Things. They only knew that they were in a big building with fluorescent lights.

Then we moved to Maine.

One of our first local shopping experiences was at a cake supply store called Cakes by Jan. It's a small, cozy store packed from floor to ceiling with everything a baker would need. What's more, the owner knows cakes. And now she knows me and my children, too. She remembers that I'm usually looking for sports-related cake decorations and that Wilton's butter-cream frosting is my favorite. My boys know Cakes by Jan when they see the black flag hanging outside the downtown storefront and see the cake molds and specialty pans in the window display. They are always eager (even six months too soon) to go inside and pick out a design for their next birthday cake.

Where was this enthusiasm when I took them shopping for cake supplies at the big craft stores in Florida?

Next we were introduced to Sprague's Nursery, a sprawling garden center on Union Street. My boys call Sprague's "the jungle with a playground" (see, they actually have names for stores now, instead of lumping them altogether as "errands") because of the swing set, pathways and bridges behind the greenhouse. They play hide-and-seek there while I shop nearby. And when it's time to check out, there are no lines and no displays of candy and soda next to the register.

Over the next year, we learned to depend on and love a host of small, one-of-a-kind stores, many of them family-owned. There is Briarpatch, a cozy one-room children's bookstore downtown; Bagel Central, a favorite breakfast spot where we are guaranteed to see someone we know; The Corner Store; Fairmount Market (another place to run into your neighbors); What's the Scoop?; and Nicky's Cruisin' Diner. Just to name a few.

And it's been my experience that because the city is filled with these personable stores where people know your name and neighbors gather to share news and talk about their families, even branches of larger, national businesses, such as Bank of America and Hannaford, don't slip into the aloof interactions that are so common in other parts of the country. The bank teller always remembers that I need three lollipops.

Sometimes, however, I wonder if people who have lived among this their entire lives realize how special it is. All over the country, small businesses have closed and made way for larger chain stores. The communities around them have lost their identity in the process.

Maine, and especially central and northern Maine, is unique in its sustainability of locally owned businesses, in part because of the neighborliness of its people (you don't go to Fairmount Market just to buy bread; you go there to talk about the weather with your neighbor, too), and therefore, it is one of the most charming, irreplaceable places we have ever been to.

Childhood memories are made in places like these. In fact, my fondest childhood memory is of drinking limeades at the small pharmacy in my grandparents' neighborhood. It was nothing special, and the drinks were cheap, but I remember being there more than I remember much else about visiting my grandparents' city. Even when I went back for a limeade as an adult, not much had changed. I recently heard that the limeade shop–pharmacy was torn down to make way for a hotel. And I thought, "Why would anyone want to reserve a room and stay there when there's no limeade shop?"

These days, my boys don't bring their handheld video games on errands anymore. Taking them to buy annuals, new books, a morning snack or candle for their birthday cake is no longer a chore. It's an experience. I had that experience only when I was on vacation visiting my grandparents. I am glad that my children are living in it.

ZUCCHINI: PLANT OF HORRORS

LAST WEEK, LINDELL AND I WENT TO SPRAGUE'S NURSERY on Union Street to pick out seeds for our second annual Smiley garden. As I spun the carousel of seed options, Lindell plucked packets from a different display across the room.

"How about these?" he asked, running toward me.

When I flipped the packet over and saw the picture on the front, my heart began to race. Zucchini. (Cue horrifying screeching sound.) "Not, not those, Lindell," I said. "Hurry, put these back where you found them."

Zucchini plants and I go way back to last year, when I first learned to garden. They are such innocent-looking seeds—flat and oval like the more familiar pumpkin seed. But out of this deceptive, smooth exterior springs one of nature's most angry and aggressive plants.

To be fair, all plants have their own personalities. Lettuce is the hard worker, consistently and inconspicuously creating layer upon layer of tasty leaves. Although prolific, lettuce has the good manners to keep to itself and, in some varieties, even to grow into a discrete, compact ball.

Sugar snap peas are the fragile, pretty ones that need constant attention. They delicately wrap themselves around a climbing pole and then sprout the most beautiful dainty white flowers, which you may never see unless you check on them daily. Just as soon as the flower bursts forth, it shrivels up and becomes a crinkly appendage, like a scrap piece of tissue paper. Still delicate and beautiful in its own way, but clearly pouting.

Corn is the showoff. It is like people who claim to eat candy bars and not gain weight. Tall and skinny, corn still somehow manages to cast a shadow on the rest of the garden, sometimes to the point of extinction for everything around it. Then it bears heavy ears of corn that seem impossible for such a lanky plant to lift. Just when you think the cornstalks can't get any taller, you lose a child in it.

Green onions, which smell of onion even as they are growing, are the loner of the group that you suspect the other vegetables are making fun of.

And carrots? Well, they don't believe in themselves. They cower in the corner, seemingly not producing much of anything at all, and then you pull them up and want to say, "You did this? You did this all by yourself?"

But zucchini—it is the angry, volatile vegetable with plans to take over the entire garden. Around the time that my zucchini plant from last year started growing prickly skin, its motives became obvious: Nothing—not me or my shovel—could stop it from growing over, around and under every neighboring plant. It would strangle the life out of its peers if needed. I doubt that a bottle of poison would have helped.

I became afraid of the zucchini. When I went to bed at night, the plant would have but one or two small green vegetables hanging from its vine. By morning, those would have tripled in size and become so deformed they looked like misshapen baseball bats. I thought the skin on them would burst, which reminded me of my fingers when I was nine months pregnant. This zucchini plant couldn't possibly be normal. Or safe.

We started receiving phone calls with no caller on the other end. If I listened closely, I could almost hear the zucchini breathing through the receiver.

"Mrs. Smiley, we have traced the call and it is coming from . . . your garden."

When I harvested the plant to use for dinner, I found myself chopping it aggressively with my kitchen knife. Sweat poured from my temples. I cleaned up all the juice and the evidence just in case the zucchini's friends would want revenge.

I eventually decided to dig up the plant to protect my family. The vines clawed at my skin, and their fat tentacles were wrapped around the sugar snap peas and the fence posts like a boa constrictor. The roots seemed to be anchored to the very center of the Earth. When I was finished, I had dirt all over my face and body, and Dustin thought I had been in a fight. I had.

Unfortunately, I left the bag of zucchini plant parts near the garden. The next morning, one of the vines was reaching out of the black plastic and fastening itself to the wooden border of the garden. It was like the hand of a zombie coming out of the grave. I shoved it back into the bag and tied it tight.

Back at Sprague's, Lindell wanted to know why we couldn't buy zucchini seeds. This is like a child asking why they can't play with a loaded gun. I told him we could get pumpkin seeds instead.

As I said earlier, however, pumpkin and zucchini seeds have unsettling similarities. So I'm keeping my eye on those guys, and I've left my shovel nearby just as a warning.

A Frozen Christmas Tree

IF YOU ARE ONE OF MY NEIGHBORS AND YOU SAW ME BLOW-drying the limbs of our Christmas tree the other night, do not panic.

You see, we have lived in Maine for nearly three years, and we still can't get this whole cutting-down-your-own-tree thing right. Which isn't to say we would be Christmas tree experts otherwise. We would not. Dustin, in particular, has a history with Christmas trees.

For instance, there was that time in Florida when he took our tree out of the house top first. Do you know what happens when you shove a large, pyramid-shaped tree through a small doorway, and you lead with the smallest part?

Each limb of the tree scraped across our red door as if it was clawing to pull itself back inside the house. One by one, the limbs bent backward like a slingshot, and then they snapped forward, taking most of the door's red paint with them.

And there were still some ornaments on the tree, too. Once the trunk had (un)successfully cleared the doorway and Dustin was plodding down the sidewalk with the tree slung over his shoulder, what was left in the front hallway looked like the scene of an accident. Even our old border collie—the one who eventually would chew a hole through our back porch—was stunned by the damage.

As soon as it was quiet again (which is to say, once there were no more tree branches digging tracks on our painted metal door, and the last fallen ornament had rolled across the tile floor and hit a stop at the wall), my dad, who was visiting at the time, said, "Well, that's one way to get a tree out of the house."

Here in Maine, it's getting the tree into the house that is a problem. It's further complicated by the fact that no one can ever hope to be a Mainer if they buy a tree that they haven't chopped down themselves, often in the middle of nowhere, when the temperature is colder than the inside of your freezer.

Speaking of freezing . . .

This year we brought home our tree, bound tight with string and netting, the night before one of the season's first snowstorms. It also was the night before I had a 20-page paper due at school. We would not be able to decorate the tree until the next day.

"So, I'll just set it outside in the snow," Dustin said. "It will get plenty of water."

I was too busy to think about what that might mean.

The next day, after the kids got home from school, we baked and frosted cookies, made spaghetti and listened to Christmas music in preparation for our tree decorating night. All the while, and unbeknownst to us, our tree was frozen solid in the backyard.

The children wrestled and fought, the way they always do when they are excited and tired of waiting, while Dustin and I got the supplies together: ornaments, lights, tree stand. We moved furniture to make room for the tree.

Then the moment that everyone had been waiting for arrived. It was time to bring in our Christmas tree. The children clapped.

Dustin came through the living room with what looked like a large missile covered in snow. We fought trying to get the trunk situated in the tree stand, and then we fought again about how close the tree could be to the wall before we snipped the string and let the limbs (theoretically) fall into place.

"It's going to scratch the wall," Dustin said.

Apparently he thought our tree was a jack-in-the-box just waiting to pounce. Then again, he saw what that tree did to our door in Florida.

"It's not going to scratch the wall," I said. "Just cut the string."

"I'm telling you, it's going to hit the wall."

"Just do it."

The kids were chanting now, too. "Cut it! Cut it!"

As Dustin slipped the scissors underneath the string, I started to have second thoughts. What if the limbs did spring forth and hit the television and lamp?

Dustin asked again. "Are you sure?"

"Just cut it!"

The final string was cut. Dustin crouched down and turned away, as if the tree would explode. I held my breath.

And here's what the tree did: nothing. It still looked like a gigantic missile covered in snow, only now it was standing vertically in a pot. The limbs were frozen solid against the trunk.

This is where the hair dryer came in. As the limbs thawed, droplets of water rained down on our hardwood floor. You could even hear the pitter-patter, just like a real storm. It would have been neat, if it weren't my house.

Eventually the tree took its ordinary shape, and the children began hanging ornaments. Dustin put his arm around me, and I smiled up at him.

"Really feels like Christmas now, doesn't it?" I asked.

And he said, "Nah, it's not Christmas until someone breaks a priceless heirloom ornament."

The Unsung Heroes of Winter

As a military dependent, I know something about sacrifices that go unnoticed. I also know something about the people who keep watch while the rest of us go about our daily lives. Often, however, I forget that this duty is shared by hundreds of other public servants, maybe not in a typical war setting, but shared nonetheless.

Last week, I was reminded of this oversight while driving behind a snowplow, in the middle of a snowstorm, on my way home from work.

I didn't know what a snowplow looked like until we moved to Maine. Actually, there was a lot that I didn't know until then. After the first significant snowstorm, Dustin and I ventured outside for an education. First: shoveling.

Lesson No. 1: If you don't lace your snow boots, you will lose one of them when you step out the door and into a foot of snow. Then you will stand on one foot like a flamingo until you find a safe, dry place (problem: After a snowstorm, there is no such place) to rest your socked foot.

Dustin and I quickly became adept at shoveling. We even enjoyed the exercise. We were struck by the friendliness of Mainers when they are outside for the post-storm cleanup. It reminded me of the days after a hurricane in Florida.

Then, while we were standing by the curb, clearing a walkway on the sidewalk, an oversize orange truck with two long, intimidating scoops on the front crept around the corner. We heard the noise—scraping on the pavement—first. Then we saw the orange blinking lights. After the truck turned and headed toward us, we noticed that the driver was waving his hands.

"Look, he's waving at us," Dustin said.

We both stood on what would have been the curb if it weren't covered in snow. We smiled and waved back at the driver.

The driver waved more frantically. As he came closer, pushing a wall of snow on the curb in front of us as he went, Dustin and I realized that the driver wasn't waving at all. He was telling us to move. I did a back dive of sorts into a snowbank. Snow rained down on my hat as the truck passed. After I got myself back up and dusted off my snow pants, I noticed the plow had pushed all the snow back onto our driveway.

Lesson No. 2: Shovel snow "downstream" from your driveway.

(Closely related lesson No. 3: Rake your roof and THEN shovel the walkway.)

Over the next few months, I grew to appreciate the sound of plows scraping past the house in the middle of the night. It was as comforting to me as the sound of jets and helicopters passing over our house in Florida or Virginia. While we slept, someone else was keeping watch.

Of course, it isn't completely fair to compare battling snow with soldiers fighting enemies. In Maine, after all, most people love the snow and see the seasonal confrontation of man vs. nature as more convivial than adversarial. With our flimsy plastic shovels, we take a stab at snow removal. Knowing that we will never fully win is part of the fun.

Still, snowplows are there for us when winter snow would otherwise disrupt daily life.

That was the case last Wednesday. I was driving home on I-95 at the height of a storm. Everything—the road, the trees, the roadside signs—was covered in white. As my wheels slipped and spun, unexpectedly sending me this way and that, I gripped the steering wheel until my knuckles were white and my fingers were numb. My speed was 15 mph. I scanned the road for melting tracks of previous cars, but there were none. I considered pulling off the side of the road.

Then, up ahead in the distance, through a fog of white, I saw orange flashing lights. A snowplow was pulling onto the interstate. The driver waited until I was closer before he slowly, cautiously pulled out in front of me.

For the next several miles, the plow cleared a path in front of me. We were like two jets flying in formation, only moving much slower. Giant waves of snow flew from the side of the truck, and ahead of me now on the road was that reassuring vision: brown, salt-laden, crumbly slush. The orange warning light on my dashboard, the one that so kindly alerts me to the fact that I'm sliding, finally went away.

When I merged right for my exit, I managed to pull up alongside the snowplow. The massive truck rose high above my van. I peered up to see out my side window, and although I was afraid to take my hands of the wheel, I nodded my head and smiled. The driver gave me a small salute. I knew what he meant: "Don't worry, we've got your back."

SMALL-TOWN LIFE

BEFORE 2008, WE ALWAYS LIVED IN A METROPOLITAN AREA. By "metropolitan area," I mean somewhere with a Cheesecake Factory within driving distance.

When we got orders to go to a small town, I told my husband, Dustin, "I'll go for two years and not a day more." Then I prepared myself for the worst.

Eight weeks after moving deep into the heart of New England, however, something strange happened. I fell in love with a place—a very small place with a relatively low median income.

"I love it, and I'm never leaving," I told Dustin.

"What happened to 'two years and not a day more'?" he asked.

Our friends back in Cheesecake Factory land started to wonder if something was wrong with me.

"You're really staying?" they asked. "But why?"

That's when I tell them what living in a small town has taught me.

1. "Unlimited options" really means "unending rat race."
In a big city, you can spend a whole day—maybe even a week—searching for just the right thing. Maybe you are looking for a living room chair, a pair of jeans or countertop for the kitchen. You go to one store and find something you

like, but your nagging subconscious says, "they might have something better at the other store."

So you go to seven more places, with long periods of traffic in between, and still you aren't sure.

That thing you're searching for is like a carrot on a stick, always just out of reach at the other store. Even after you settle on a chair, jeans or countertop, you suffer from buyer's remorse: "If I'd just searched longer, I probably could have gotten something better, cheaper."

And the worst part is that everyone around you has the same unlimited options. So everyone keeps getting more and better things.

In a small town, if the one mall on Main Street doesn't have it, you probably don't need it.

2. Small towns love their downtowns.

Speaking of Main Street: There's a reason Cheesecake Factory doesn't exist in small towns. Sure, maybe the economy can't support them, but the residents might not either. Mom-and-pop stores and restaurants still exist in small town America, and the people who live there love them. In fact, they probably know the owner.

3. It's about who you are, not what you do.

For most of my early adult life, people were introduced to me as "CEO of such-and-such." I knew people by what they did, not who they were. Life was fragmented between "work" and "home." I went to the dentist, but I never would have known his family.

In a small town, it's impossible not to know your dentist's family. You probably knew them before you showed up for an appointment. You also probably know the dental hygienist and the receptionist. Maybe your kids are on the same basketball team. Maybe they live down the street. Either way, the fact that they are "the receptionist" or "the dentist" is a mere footnote to you. When you go home and talk about your day, you refer to them by name, not their title.

4. In the absence of "things to do," you get to know other people.

"But what do you DO there?" friends like to ask.

I understand their concern. Until I moved to a small town, I wouldn't have known what to do without three-leveled malls, state-of-the-art movie theaters and world-renowned golf courses. I could spend a whole day doing errands or shuttling the kids to planned activities.

But it turns out that all those things are just distractions.

In the absence of what popular culture considers "things to do," small-town America is getting to know its neighbors. In the summer, they sit on their front sidewalk and talk to one another. While outside shoveling snow, they stand in the street and talk. When they find your dog roaming in their backyard, they bring him home. They call you when your son is out on his bike after the street lights have gone out.

5. Everyone knows everyone else.

Admittedly, small-town life is not for everyone. Most people cite the inability to be anonymous as the main reason they couldn't live in a small place. True, sometimes you just want to go to the grocery store and not see anyone you know. But when it really counts, a small town is there for you.

Last month, a family in our small town experienced a tragedy after their son died. People set up an online account to raise a modest amount of money for them. They raised six-times that from hundreds of small donations, and they did it in two days.

Which perhaps is the greatest power of a small town: Your life touches and is touched by everyone, not for the possessions you have, the places you shop or what you do but for who you are and because you belong.

APOLOGIES TO THE WILDLIFE

NOTE: No ANIMALS WERE HARMED IN THE FOLLOWING accounts. But no animals were left untouched, uninspected or unstudied either. It is the author's belief that the best way for children to gain an appreciation for nature is to interact with it.

SECOND NOTE: One child was harmed by an animal during the following accounts.

To the robin that built a nest outside our door while we were on vacation:

In our absence, I'm sure the wooden beam in our tree-filled backyard seemed safe and accommodating. You probably didn't even notice the lightsabers beneath you, or the water blasters stacked on the bench. And I can see how those brightly colored balls might have been confusing. Did they look like flowers or vegetables?

Indeed, when we came home, we were shocked to see the mess of your nest—scattered grass and droppings of mud—on our back porch.

"A bird made a nest here?" I said. "What was she thinking?"

Just then, you looked down, and I was sure you were making angry faces at me. A short 10 minutes later, the boys ran through the back door like bulls released from pens. They took up their lightsabers and chased each other. The youngest one blasted potted plants with water from his gun. And although I asked them to stay away from your area, let's face it, their voices can be heard a mile away.

When your mate returned with food and the two of you scuffled in a nearby pine tree, I knew what you were saying: "You expect me to live here? What kind of bird do you think I am?"

Don't worry, the worst the boys will do is stare at you through binoculars, make chirping sounds near your nest and scatter what they think you'd like to eat (frozen waffles?) around the yard. They mean well.

To the frogs with funny names:

It's called a net, that thing with holes in it and with a long green handle on one end. Hop into the net and you're a goner. Unless you enjoy a brief stay in a frog aquarium, where a 4-year-old will press his nose against the glass and give you funny names until his parents convince him to let you go, or you evolve before our eyes and escape. (I'll have you know, Hoppy Donut Frog, Lindell cried all the way home about your sneaky getaway. And when we found the bullfrog later, Lindell squealed, "Look at how much Hoppy Donut Frog has grown!")

But the bullfrog (named Hoppy Cookie Frog), well, he's the one you should feel sorry for. The boys built the Roman Colosseum out of sand, filled it with water and tried to find another bullfrog for Hoppy Cookie to battle. While the children ate lunch, Dustin let Hoppy Cookie free. He seemed disappointed.

To the butterfly named Flying Butter:

Oh, Flying Butter! Owen caught you on his pinkie finger and you stayed for almost an hour. He ate with you there, fed the ducks with you there and even ran through the backyard with you there. You were like a decorative ring on his finger. You could have left at any moment, but you chose to stay (even when that dragonfly landed on Owen's other hand). When it was finally your time to leave, you caught the wind, and we watched you fly across the lake. Owen was both sad and happy.

To the fish with multiple hooks in its mouth:

"Mom, we caught another bass!" they yelled. "Mom, we caught a bass AGAIN!"

That's when I knew something was up. My dad had been fishing several nights for bass. He caught only one. How had the boys caught multiple gigantic bass in just an hour?

I went to the dock and discovered a nest of baby bass under the water. The boys' "big fish" was protecting babies. I told the boys to leave that spot alone, and they were delighted when days later we found billions of teeny little black fish. (They scooped up one in a net, of course.)

Unfortunately, somewhere in the lake there is a big bass with several hooks in its mouth who curses my children and the day their dad showed them how to cast a line.

To the leech who caught a boy:

Appreciation sometimes means trapping a frog and then realizing it really wants to be set free. Or, watching a bird fly away because you've been too noisy. And, learning that you can't keep a butterfly.

Granted, all of these lessons come at the expense of some wildlife's peace and quiet. But education (on both sides) also comes from pain and torment inflicted by wildlife.

When Lindell chased a flock of ducks through the weeds, you, Mr. Leech, took the opportunity to feast on his little toe. Boy, were you surprised, and suddenly more educated, when you emerged from the water and realized what you had caught! I'm not sure who was more shocked: Lindell with a bloodsucking black slug on his toe, or the bloodsucker that had a screaming 4-year old boy stuck to its mouth.

My bet is on the bloodsucker.

THE MOTHER BIRD

A MOTHER ROBIN MADE A NEST OUTSIDE OUR KITCHEN door. It wasn't a great choice as far as locations go. I'm sure she realizes that now. But we were on vacation at the time, so how could she have known?

Over the last month, as I've watched the robin perfect her nest, lay eggs in it, incubate them and then, finally, feed the babies (she even has three—I'm sure they are boys), I've felt a deep kinship with her.

First, I watched as she sat on the newly created nest and struggled with her eggs. Maybe this was just my imagination. Everything I've read indicates that female birds do not gain weight when they have an egg, nor do they feel pain when they lay it. (Of course, everything I've read was probably written by a man.) Still, I'm quite sure the mother robin looked plump and uncomfortable the day before I climbed a ladder and spotted a new blue egg in her nest. Her chest was squished against her neck ("Lie down," I wanted to tell her. "It's the only way to keep everything where it should be: not in your throat."), and she was breathing heavily with her beak wide open. I bet her ankles were swollen.

We shared a moment when the robin looked through the window at me sitting at the kitchen table. Again, maybe this was my imagination, but she seemed angry at the male robin in a tree nearby. And well she should be! I nodded to show my empathy. I was like the compassionate nurse who knows that the daddy bird just doesn't get it.

A few days later, the robin sat on her eggs and stayed there to incubate them. I shooed kids away from the area and tried to give the mom a large radius of calm and quiet. I worried that seeing my children with lightsabers and swords might make the mother second-guess her decision to start a family. "They aren't all like this," I wanted to say. "I've witnessed kids who sit and color. Really, I have! But, well, you need opposable thumbs for that."

Another two weeks passed, and suddenly a tiny gray, fuzzy head popped up from the nest. The babies had been born! One by one, they opened their beaks and swayed back and forth, eager for a worm. Persistent little beggars.

It was around this time that my relationship with the mother began to change. It's the same with human women: We commiserate over pregnancies, but once the babies are born, it's every mom for herself: "My stroller is bigger than yours, and I feed my baby only organic."

Maybe it was the way I always swept away the robin's mess—pieces of grass and twigs that fell from the nest. Perhaps she thought my actions were saying something. Or maybe it was the drip from our window air conditioner that coincidentally fell just a few feet away from the nest. More likely, however, our rift can be blamed on that time I saw the mother bird sit on her babies.

I was reading the morning paper, and I heard the baby birds peeping just outside the screen door. They were swaying again, begging for food. The mother flew back and forth, busily presenting one morsel for each mouth. But the babies kept peeping and swaying. The mother could not fly fast enough.

Then all at once, while one baby still had its head resting on the edge of the nest, the mother sat on her babies. The peeping and swaying stopped. The birds gave up and went to sleep.

The mother looked at me and I at her. Her face was indignant. Mine, accusing. I had become that mother at Walmart who gawks and shakes her head while another parent disciplines her child.

The robin continued to stare at me. I knew what she was saying:

"Yeah, I'd like to see you try to feed three babies all at once. I don't have thumbs, or tools, or even a monogamous mate. And these babies! They just keep begging and begging. Their swaying never stops. They're fighting and pushing each other in the nest. I can't even comfortably fit in here with them. Judge me and I'll judge you: I saw your 4-year-old eat two packages of fruit snacks in a row. And your 10-year-old? Well, he doesn't wash his hands before dinner. And does your middle son eat anything else besides peanut butter?"

I reminisced about the robin's pregnancy, when she and I were a team, when we understood each other.

Later that day, my family gathered at the dinner table for a meal. The bird nest was just outside the screen door. My boys were exceptionally hungry. I went back and forth from the stove to the table with multiple helpings for them. I hardly had a chance to sit down myself.

I looked out the window at the robin. She looked back. "Bet you wish you could just sit on them," she said.

One Bird in the House is Worse Than Two Outside

I HAD A DEAL WITH THE MOTHER ROBIN WHO HAS MADE A nest outside our kitchen window for the last four years. That deal included things like, "I'll stop judging your parenting if you stop judging mine," and, "Mind your own business; I've got three birds—I mean, kids—in here, OK? And they don't eat worms."

It also included me rescuing baby birds from the jaws of Sparky, our 2-year-old Brittany spaniel, who loves to hunt. I did this once, famously, while former MLB pinch-hitter Matt Stairs was visiting for Dinner with the Smileys. While Stairs and the children watched an MLB Bloopers DVD, I had a life-or-death situation on my hands in the backyard. No one in the living room ever knew anything was amiss.

My agreement with the mother bird, however, never included anything about her brood being allowed inside our house. (Note: I don't go in her nest either.) And that's why things got a little tense between us last week.

The robin, by the way, must be a fertile little thing, because she has several clutches in one summer. From June to late August she slaves over different sets of eggs. She always uses the same nest, in the same location, and I have a front-row seat from my kitchen table. Over and over again, at least three times a summer, I grieve as her fuzzy, gray-headed babies leave. (Oh, how she must hate me when she looks in the window and sees mine still there!)

Her last nest is usually in August. This year, though, it seemed like it might be a dud. I never heard the familiar chirps of the babies, nor did I see their spiky hair sticking up over the edges of the nest. I didn't even see the mother going maniacally back and forth with worms hanging from her mouth.

Last week, I found out why: the mother robin had herself an only child.

One lonely little bird poked his head from the nest last week, and then he stood up and took a look around. This is always my cue that the birds, or bird, will soon fledge. Usually, I lock Sparky inside the house so he won't nab the baby before it's had a chance.

But last week, my mother-in-law, also named Robin, oddly enough, was visiting from Seattle, and I forgot to give her the lowdown on my relationship with the birds. I told her that a baby was going to fly soon, but I forgot to mention that we should leave Sparky inside. Oops.

All of the sudden, while I was upstairs brushing my hair, I heard a horrible fuss outside. The mother bird was squawking and swooping between the trees. Sparky's dog tags jingled, and his nails gripped the wooden deck.

I knew he had gotten a bird.

Before I could even put down my brush, I heard Robin—the person, not the bird—screaming from downstairs, "Sparky got a bird and brought it inside the house! There's a bird inside the house!"

I ran down the stairs and found Sparky standing over a teeny, shivering bird on our living room floor. He couldn't have been prouder. With an open-mouth grin and a tail that moved his entire backside, he seemed to be saying, "Look, I got your dinner!"

I knew the bird wasn't hurt because Sparky holds them with a characteristically "soft mouth." He never intends to eat them. They are "gifts" for me, his mom, if you will. But I had seen the mess these birds make on my back porch, and it was just a matter of time before this one pooped on the carpet.

My mother-in-law was still screaming. She wanted Ford, 12, to catch the bird in a sheet and take him outside. Meanwhile, Ford and his younger brothers had locked themselves in my bedroom. It was just me, the baby bird, one happy dog, and a frantic Robin (the person, not the bird).

I got a towel, scooped up the bird and walked to the back porch. Sparky's tail stopped wagging as he followed. "Um, you aren't going to just let that one go, are you?" he seemed to be saying.

I put the baby bird in the grass and shooed Sparky back into the house. Then I stood on the deck and shook my finger at the mother.

"Did you have to let it fly while my door was open?" I asked her. "Your timing is lousy, you know. You nearly gave my mother-in-law a heart attack. And the children! Next time, wait until I'm ready, OK?"

The mother swiveled her head in that pretentious, unblinking way birds do.

I sighed and went back inside.

When I looked out the door later, the mother and the baby were gone. Already, I couldn't wait to see her again next year.

Raising Kids in Maine

THE NEW (NAUGHTY) KID IN CLASS

AFTER THE FIRST FEW DAYS IN A NEW CLASSROOM, ESPE-cially if it is in a new school in a new state, your child is likely to come home and claim he doesn't know the names of any other students.

"You can't remember even one friend's name?" you'll say, desperate for all the details. But your child's lips are sealed. Only after your relentless prodding will your child finally confess: "Well, there is this *one* kid . . ."

That "one kid," the only student whose name your son or daughter knows, is guaranteed to be the naughty kid.

Every class has a naughty kid (remember that; it's important later). Other children quickly learn the naughty kid's name because they hear it called aloud by the teacher—with various undertones of anger and frustration—over and over again. Beware any child whose name is the first one that your son or daughter learns, especially if your child says this person is his new best friend.

But what if your child *is* the naughty kid? How will you know?

Your first clue might be if your son or daughter says there isn't a naughty student in the class. (Remember, there is *always* a naughty kid.)

ME (speaking to my 5-year-old son, who just started kin-dergarten): "Owen, did you learn any friends' names today?"

OWEN: "No, Mom."

ME: "Not even the naughty kid's name? Your older brother always learned the naughty kid's name on the first day."

OWEN: "We don't have a naughty kid in our class."

ME: "No naughty kid? That's impossible. Every class has a naughty kid."

OWEN: "Not my class."

ME: "Well that's good. But you don't know anyone's name? You didn't hear the teacher say someone's name over and over again?"

OWEN: "Nope."

The second clue that your child is the naughty one in his class: Other parents know your child's name.

ANOTHER PARENT: "You're Owen's mom, right?"

ME: "Yes."

ANOTHER PARENT: "We hear a lot about Owen."

The third and final clue that your child is the naughty one in class: They seem to always have a new seat.

ME: "Owen, what was your favorite part of the week?"

OWEN: "That I'm sitting at my friend's table again."

ME: "You've switched tables already? It's only the second week of school."

OWEN: "I switch tables every day, Mom. Each time I get in trouble, the teacher finds me a new seat."

I was shocked when I finally put it all together. I didn't want my child—my Owen—to be "that kid." I didn't want him to be the naughty one. When I talked to my husband, Dustin, about it, he chuckled and said, "Owen has come a long way. Do you remember when he wouldn't talk at all? Do you remember how you worried that he would always be shy?"

Dustin is right. Just two years ago, our Owen, who has always been in the third percentile for weight, was a scrawny 4-year-old boy who couldn't keep even size-2T pants on his hips. He seldom talked, and he cried every time I left him at preschool. He had trouble making friends.

Now our pint-size little boy—the one we used to call "Tiny Tim"—has blossomed into someone who apparently can't *stop* making friends—even during circle time and rest time. And while it's nice to see him growing, that doesn't mean he can misbehave.

"I guess I need to call Owen's teacher and arrange a meeting," I said that night, and my oldest son, Ford, overheard.

"I bet the teacher will answer and say, 'Well, hello there, you naughty parent'," Ford said, bringing a whole new element into my dilemma. If every class has a naughty child, I guess it makes sense that there is a "naughty parent" as well.

Owen came into the room and heard us talking. "Oh, come on now, stop," he said. "Let's not go calling my teacher or anything. I've got it all under control."

Which, of course, is Clue No. 1 that you need a parent-teacher conference pronto.

GIFT SHOPS = HELL

IT WAS A LOVELY DAY SPENT AT A MINIATURE RAILWAY VILlage and museum with my children and parents during their annual summer visit. The weather was perfect, and the location offered something for everyone.

Dad enjoyed a classic cars display and historical train facts. Mom browsed antiques. The kids saw a model train being built, the skeleton of its tracks and plaster mountains still unpainted and fully exposed as if through X-ray. We even took a train ride, where a cool breeze blew our hair back and especially delighted Lindell, 2.

On the way out of the railway village, however, we met a familiar foe: the gift store. Dustin's philosophy is that families go into gift stores feeling jubilant and expectant, but leave in tears and with empty pockets. For him, gift stores are not happy places. Everything is overpriced, and the shelves are stocked with things our kids normally would not care about, but now, just because the pencil or backpack bears the name of the place we've just visited, they act as if leaving empty-handed will be as painful as chewing off their left arm. Even the name—gift shop—is deceiving. It implies that someone will give you a complimentary gift for having visited their park.

Ordinarily, to avoid this misery, Dustin and I bypass gift stores. But businesses have wised up to this largely universal tactic, and now many of them force you through the gift store in order to exit the park. I wouldn't put it past Dustin to live at the National Zoo indefinitely rather than go through the exit that is only accessible via the gift shop. When he finally is forced into a gift shop, Dustin's look of horror suggests that he doesn't see rows upon rows of stuffed bears and pencils with feathers stuck on the end, but instead, angry merchandise that sneers and spits at him as he passes.

It's as if all the knickknacks are saying, "And you thought admission was expensive; wait until you see how much it's gonna cost you to get out of this place."

On this occasion, however, while visiting the railway museum with my parents, Dustin and I reluctantly agreed to take our begging children into the gift shop, but only because Grandma was paying. As much as I tease, I have to hand it to Dustin; it did seem like there was a fun vacuum on either side of the entrance that sucked away all of our good humor and our children's common sense. This being a railway village, the store was filled with Thomas the Tank Engine paraphernalia. Our oldest boys—Ford, 8, and Owen, 6—haven't played with Thomas in years. Now they thought their hearts would break if they didn't have an engine named James.

"You guys don't even play with trains anymore," I said.

"But we will. We promise. Please, pretty please."

The woman behind the counter witnessed my boys' meltdown with sympathy all over her face. With her lips, she mouthed "I'm sorry" to me. If I hadn't looked away, I think she might have gone on to say, "I just work here part time. Don't blame me. Look I'm a mom, too. If it were up to me, there would be no gift shops anywhere. Not ever."

Now Owen was crying as if his pet just died, and Ford had resorted to his default: accusing us of favoring Lindell "just because he's the baby."

How did a happy family outing suddenly turn into an angry, dysfunctional therapy session in the middle of a store? Dustin had had enough. He walked out the front door and onto the store's porch, where he found my dad, hands in pockets, whistling up at the sky. Dad didn't want to know how much money Mom was spending. He didn't want to know if the kids were behaving. It seemed that he wanted to pretend none of it was happening at all, and he wished only that everyone made it out alive.

More than $50 later, Mom and I came out of the store with the boys following at our heels. They were still sniffling and wiping away tears, even as they each held a sack with a new toy inside.

Lindell was so excited to see the car waiting to take him home, he dropped his new train on the ground like a rag and hopped into his car seat.

"You've got to be kidding me," Dustin said. "We're never going into another gift shop. They're nothing but one big money pit, and look, the boys don't even care about what they get there." He pointed at the train on the ground.

Dustin was being nice. Because I was thinking, at that very moment, that gift shops are more along the lines of the eighth circle of hell.

KIDS AS COLLATERAL AT THE COUNTY FAIR

SOUVENIR GIFT SHOPS ARE PROOF TO DUSTIN THAT EVIL does exist. He calls them "fun vacuums," and he would rather live the rest of his life trapped inside a petting zoo than leave through a strategically placed gift shop that doubles as a park's only exit.

Asking Dustin to purchase an overpriced bobblehead can turn this normally calm man with exceptionally low blood pressure into Jack Torrance from Stephen King's *The Shining*. Dustin is that guy in the middle of the souvenir shop who looks like he's suffering from a heart attack when he says, "You've got to be kidding me? Five dollars for this piece of junk?"

So you can imagine how Dustin feels about county fairs, especially the kind that no longer center on local agriculture, but have mushroomed to include an overwhelming sideshow of rides, cheap toys and overpriced food. Once, when we lived in Florida, I desperately wanted to pay a dollar to "step right up and see the head of a woman on the body of a snake" at the county fair. I thought Dustin would leave me at the suggestion. Eventually, however, he reasoned that it would be educational for me to see how Americans spend their hard-earned money.

I walked up a metal ramp and onto a platform. Below me in a black box was a giant rubber snake folded onto itself in several coils. Its head had been cut off. In its place was the head of a woman whose body was hidden behind a black curtain. I couldn't decide which was worse, the fact that this woman agreed to be the head of a snake, or the fact that I had paid to see it. I covered my mouth with my hand and walked down the ramp. I thought I might vomit. Dustin was visibly pleased as he put out an arm to hug me. He was sure I would never spend money at a fair again.

Then we had children. It is one of life's great mysteries that kids (the same ones who scream about a spider on their bedroom wall) are attracted by a force greater than themselves to things that defy humanity, such as costumed individuals with giant round heads that wobble on their shoulders.

Last week, when the fair came to town, our children begged to visit it, and we took them despite knowing that not one of the three boys would ride on a single attraction. We paid our $40 total admission price for the privilege of walking around a parking lot in the blazing heat, explaining to the children in a continuous loop why we wouldn't pay more than $1 for a cup of lemonade, and why fried dough with powdered sugar does not qualify as "lunch." When Dustin learned that our admission included unlimited rides for the whole day, he called a family huddle and said, "I'm not leaving this park until we have gone on $40 worth of rides."

The kids said, "We just want to buy souvenirs."

We passed a kiosk selling $10 lightsabers, and the begging began. Dustin and I were a powerful, unified wall of

"No" until Ford pulled out a $20 bill from his pocket and said, "We'll buy it with our own money."

"If you want to waste your money on a cheap toy that will be broken tomorrow, go ahead," Dustin said. And Ford and Owen did. But Lindell, 3, didn't have his own money, so he couldn't get a light saber. We were reminded of this with ear-piercing screams for the next seven days.

Eventually my mom gave Lindell $10 to get his own. This was about six days after Owen's lightsaber broke. So on a hot afternoon, I walked three miles from my home to the fair, with Lindell in the stroller and Owen by my side, to buy a new lightsaber and replace a broken one. Only, I wouldn't pay $30 admission to do it. At the first entrance, I explained my situation to the staff: "I just need to go to the light saber kiosk and then we'll come right back out."

The guard studied me. "How can I be sure you won't ride any rides?"

"Because I'm with a 7- and 3-year-old who were too afraid to ride anything the first time I paid $40," I said.

Then, in a stunning move, the guard said, "You'll have to leave the child [nodding at Owen] here while you go inside."

Basically, he wanted to keep my 7-year-old as collateral. For a brief second, I considered the idea. That's how desperate I had become. I hadn't walked three miles in the heat for nothing. Then I thought better. Leave my kid? Seriously? Just how crazy did this man think I was?

I thought about this on my way to the next entrance in search of a new, better answer, like "Sure, come on through, but make it quick." That's when it occurred to me. I looked just about as a crazy as a woman who would walk three miles to buy a $10 lightsaber that would break tomorrow. Shoot, I probably even looked like the kind of woman who would pay $1 to see the head of a woman on the body of a snake.

Frozen Waffles
(Hey, I cook them first!)

Mornings—especially school mornings—are a particularly chaotic time when you have three young children. Much of the chaos centers on breakfast. And by "breakfast," I mean "frozen waffles," because in our house, there is no distinction. By the time my children are grown, I will have prepared an absurd amount of frozen waffles. If only my boys could gain an appetite for a different kind of breakfast, one that doesn't involve standing at the toaster oven for three minutes, three times in a row, and then buttering six waffles and making three bowls of syrup for dipping.

Six years ago, I thought the emerging waffles-for-breakfast routine was just a phase. I figured it would disappear and then come again, like the boys' cyclical taste for tacos or peanut butter sandwiches. I was wrong. At this point, if you take into account the rare instances in which we have temporarily run out of frozen waffles, an emergency situation to be discussed below, I figure that I have prepared approximately 10,220 waffles.

What is cyclical, however, is the boys' preference for waffle type and preparation, so we have developed our own code words to differentiate. "Regular waffles" are the standard variety. Owen likes these with butter only and syrup on the side for dipping. Ford likes them buttered but prefers to add his own syrup, which is always too much. Owen likes his cut in two; Ford not at all.

"Square waffles" are the miniature waffles that are technically cinnamon toast. They can be broken apart into four separate squares and that's the way Ford likes them. But if you dare break apart Owen's serving, he will flop onto the ground like a seal that has underestimated the jump onto a rock.

"Waffle sticks" are actually French toast that can be broken into four sticks. Both Ford and Owen like them served whole so that they can break them and dip them into a bowl of syrup.

You probably noticed that I didn't mention Lindell, our youngest, and his preferences. That's because Lindell will eat anything, in any presentation, and therefore he usually receives all the cut-up, mashed-up, broken-apart waffles that were unsuitable to his brothers.

Now, if the wrong waffle presentation is enough to make Owen flop on the ground, you can imagine the calamity of not having any waffles at all. Ford and Lindell, who are usually pretty understanding about waffle mistakes, can be reduced to fits of rage on the mornings that we discover we have run out of frozen waffles. Because Owen previously has been so dramatic about ill-prepared waffles, he has but one last resort in these crises: not to eat at all. In fact, he will hardly speak if he can't have waffles.

So you can see the predicament Dustin and I faced Wednesday morning when we opened the freezer and realized that there were only two servings of "waffle sticks" left.

Three boys. Two servings. Lindell had already spotted the box and was dancing around the kitchen singing, "Waffle sticks, waffle sticks, we eat waffle sticks," which effectively laid his claim to at least one of the servings. Ford and Owen were both upstairs, completely unaware of the waffle dilemma unfolding in the kitchen.

Dustin and I knew what we had to do, and we knew it wouldn't be easy. It would, in fact, be one of those difficult decisions all parents dread. We'd have to choose between our two children. One would get waffle sticks, the other would not.

We weighed our options. Owen probably could not handle the heartbreak of watching his brothers eat waffles while he had none. We feared that he would slide off his seat, onto the floor, and perhaps curl up into a ball and never eat again. Ford would be disappointed, sure, but he usually is able to grasp the larger picture. And he never chooses not to eat.

Dustin put the waffle sticks in the toaster oven and began making a different breakfast for Ford. Lindell was still singing, "Waffle sticks, waffle sticks, we eat waffle sticks."

The older boys came downstairs to eat. Dustin decided to overcompensate for the impending tragedy by being super-cheerful and accommodating. "Do you want some milk, Ford? How about orange juice, Owen?"

The children sat down at the table. No one noticed anything awry. Not even Ford, who was devouring his meal. Then Lindell started singing again. "Waffle sticks, waffle sticks, we eat waffle sticks." Ford looked at his brothers' plates and dropped his fork.

"Hey, that's not fair!" he said. "They have waffle sticks."

"And there aren't anymore," Dustin said. "There were only two servings."

"So why didn't you ask me if I wanted waffle sticks instead of them?"

And Dustin said, "Because we were afraid that you would say yes."

National Waffle Shortage

When I wrote last week's column, I sincerely had no idea that Eggo, the frozen waffle company, is in the midst of a nationwide shortage. I had, of course, noticed that the waffle section of our grocery store was bare, save for a friendly note attached to the shelf that read: "We are working to restock this item," but I didn't realize conditions were the same elsewhere across the country. For about a month, I have been unable to buy my boys the Eggo waffles they love and was left with no option but to buy the store-brand version, which went over like a frozen stack of waffles.

The thought occurred to me, however briefly, that there might in fact be an explanation for why the waffle shelf for so long has looked like the bread and water aisles before a hurricane, and one night, on my way home from the grocery store, I had the idea to Google it. Oh, but that's so silly, I thought. How could there be a waffle shortage? I experienced a gasoline shortage in Florida after Hurricane Ivan, and the refrigerated cookie dough shelf was vacant after that salmonella scare a few months ago, but waffles? What catastrophe could possibly cause a waffle shortage?

I knew that I had more pressing matters to Google, such as why my children won't eat oatmeal, so by the time I got inside the house and unloaded the groceries, I had already forgotten about the missing waffles. Perhaps I also chose not to pursue the mystery of the empty frozen breakfast shelf because to do so would expose me as the kind of mother who doesn't fix her children eggs and toast in the morning. When Dustin asked me for waffle status updates, he did so out of the corner of his mouth: "Any word on when the you-know-whats will be back at the store?" We never mentioned the dilemma to our friends, although I suspect the scarcity of waffles was a pink elephant in the room at many a parental gathering over the last few weeks.

Then I outed our family in my column as the waffle-lovers that we are. And readers surprised me with links to news about Eggo's nationwide shortage. Apparently, the company's plant in Atlanta was shut down in September after record amounts of rain flooded the area. And in Rossville, Tenn., home of the company's largest bakery, many of the production lines are closed for repairs. With output crippled by the closures, Eggo estimates that it will be summer 2010 before supplies around the country reach their normal levels.

Some readers also surprised me with a scolding for feeding my children such "poison." (Imagine if these readers knew what my kids sometimes eat for dinner! No, not real poison, but close to it: chicken tenders and fries.) One claimed that a persistent theme is emerging in my column: My children flop on the floor when they don't get their way. So let me take this opportunity to clarify. Only one of our children is a floor flopper. The youngest prefers to slap and scream, and the oldest just says "WHAT?!?!" in a high-pitched whine that is more offensive to my ears than the sound of two marbles rubbing together. Which is to say, fear not, worried reader; we have the whole realm of disobedience here at the Smiley house.

Incidentally, our floor flopper, who shall from this point forward remain nameless, was teased by one of his peers about my column, and he has requested to never again appear on these pages. (There goes a fifth of my writing material.) I suggested he tell the teaser that while he (the teaser) was up reading the newspaper before school, my son (the flopper) was playing Wii. That's right, not only do I feed my children waffles for breakfast, I let them play Wii in the morning, too. So far, aside from the flopping, slapping and whining, they seem well-adjusted.

But back to the waffles. According to NPR, Eggo company spokeswoman Kris Charles stated in an e-mail that "the existing stock of Eggos will be distributed nationally based on stores' sales histories of the waffles." Meaning: Stores that sell the most will receive the most. You can thank me later if you live near me and our grocery store restocks some of the precious remaining waffles.

A waffle shortage. Who would have thought? Certainly not the readers who believe frozen breakfast is poison. I take comfort in the fact that for a nationwide shortage to make headline news means that I'm not the only one who has noticed. Maybe even I'm not the only one with kids flopping on the floor. (Perhaps I will attach a Swiffer duster to him until the waffles return full force in the summer.) Empty waffle shelves across the country clearly mean that I am not alone at the toaster oven.

MOMS DON'T HAVE FAVORITES

IT'S BEEN BROUGHT TO MY ATTENTION BY SEVERAL SOURCES (not one of them Owen) that I write about Ford and Lindell more than I write about my middle son. I'd like to correct that today.

It's true, I haven't written about Owen recently. But for good reason. After I referred to him as the "Waffle Flopper" earlier this year, Owen requested that I not write about him ever again. "Don't even mention my name," he said.

"I won't use 'Owen,' but can I call you the Waffle Flopper?" I asked.

Owen glared at me.

"How about just WF?"

In time, the Waffle-Flopper debacle faded from memory, and Owen has once again given me the green light to write about him.

When Owen was a baby, I called him my little "kitten." He was so small and bendy, if he ever fell from the couch, I was sure he would flip around in the air and land on his hands and knees with his back arched. He had fine, wispy hair that stood straight up in all directions. This earned him the nickname "Rooster," and although most of his hair has finally settled down, even today there is one tuft that sticks up in the back. When Owen draws pictures of himself, he is sure to include this.

Owen didn't walk or talk for a very long time. The doctors were concerned and ran all sorts of tests on him. He was so underweight, his numbers didn't register on the growth chart at the doctor's office. It was a big deal when Owen turned 5 years old and finally made it into the 3rd percentile for height and weight.

Through all of this, however, somehow I knew that my little Owen was observing everything, taking it in and becoming a better person for it. One night, when Owen was almost 2 years old, he stood up and took his first steps. Before we could even say, "Did he just walk?" Owen was doing laps around the couch. And he has been like that ever since: watching and absorbing, mastering an ability in his mind first and then surprising everyone when he finally does it. Owen cried before the first day of first grade because he didn't want to read out loud. Not yet. We thought he couldn't read at all. A few weeks later, he was reading whole books to us.

The challenges Owen has faced, and the struggles he's been through, have culminated to make him a sensitive little boy who worries so much about other people he sometimes rubs his upper lip raw from an anxious tic that involves dragging the palm of his hand from the bottom of his nose up his forehead. The night that Lindell ate a Glade PlugIns air freshener and was taken to the hospital, my friend who stayed with the boys said Owen cried in his bed for at least an hour. More recently, at a children's museum in Rockland, I watched as Owen helped a little girl who was confused by a puzzle. "Picture it in your mind," he told her. "If you put this piece there, will the ball fit through it?" He was as skillful and patient as a kindergarten teacher.

In fact, Owen is so concerned with other people's feelings, he is sometimes surprised when he receives anything for himself. My friend Susan gave the boys gumballs one day, and instead of eating his, Owen saved it like a precious stone. He kept it on the shelf above his bed and referred to it as "the one that Mrs. Stephenson gave me."

Add to this the image of Owen's smile, which always involves squinting, eyelashes that curl at the corners and eyebrows like two upside down parentheses, and you will know why I sometimes describe Owen as a ball of sunshine. Ford says that Owen has "sparklies in his eyes," and draws pictures of him with starbursts next to the eyeballs. It is impossible not to smile when Ford is taking himself too seriously, worrying about the rules of a game or the score, and Owen says, "I just tooted," then collapses on the floor giggling. Even Ford will grin.

And yet, for all the ways Owen has grown and changed, he still is the one who wants to sit in my lap and rest his head on my shoulder. He is less like a kitten these days; more like a fledgling deer with lanky, awkward legs and large feet. His face is filling out, his hair calming down. And when he's not flopping on the ground protesting the morning waffles, Owen is the happiest kid I know.

If Otters Read Books About Us

My middle son, Owen, 7, recently learned to read. For homework each night, he reads aloud a book that he is working on at school. Yesterday, the book was about a baby otter searching for food. First he tries to eat an old, crushed soda can. Owen paused here to tell us that "littering is bad." I beamed at my ecoconscious son. And then he said: "I've seen what litter can do on 'SpongeBob SquarePants.'"

Eventually, the baby otter finds a clamshell that is closed tight. He dives back to the ocean floor, just like his mother has taught him, to find a rock. Then back to the surface of the water he goes with the rock and clamshell clutched under his arms. He rolls onto his back, places the rock on his belly, and slams the clamshell against the rock until it breaks open.

"That's a lot of work just to get some food," I said when Owen had finished reading.

Owen left the room to put the book in his backpack. I watched him walk away and considered the fact that I had just returned from the grocery store. It's a feat not unlike a baby otter struggling with a clamshell, searching for a rock, and then toting the rock and shell through the water so that he can smash one against the other.

Does the otter ever think, "There has to be a better way. Like, can't I order this stuff on Amazon?"

I turned to the sink to finish washing dishes and I began to wonder: What would a baby otter think of human grocery shopping? If an otter brought home a book about it to read to his mother, might it go something like this:

The female human tries to grow food in the backyard, but this proves to be complicated because she lacks something humans call a "green thumb." Most people like eggs, milk, beef and poultry, and yet they do not keep the animals that provide such things. So the human female travels several times a week to a place called the grocery store. Grocery stores sell all the foods that humans eat, no matter where they live. Yes, there are bananas in Maine.

When the human female visits the grocery store, she usually has her children with her. The children will sit in or hang from something called a shopping cart. If the female shops at a kid-friendly store with shopping carts made to look like race cars and/or trucks, the children might even ride on top of the hood of the plastic car.

Besides the children, the shopping cart also holds all of the purchases so that the female's arms are free to pluck more food from the shelves. When the female isn't looking, the children toss unwanted and unhealthy items like Fruit Roll-Ups and Lucky Charms into the basket. If the female is lucky, that is the worst her children will do; it is not unheard of for human children to throw themselves on the floor, at the feet of their mother, and beg for candy and soda.

Sometimes, small human children dart away, duck behind a display of bread and then dash off to the frozen foods, so that the female has to sprint up and down the aisles calling out his name, and then eventually, once she finds the little rascal, backtrack through aisles 3 through 11 again to find her shopping cart, which has probably by now been emptied and returned to the front of the store by an employee.

The female usually has a portable phone in her purse, and she will use it at aisle 9 to call her husband and ask what kind of beer he wants. When he tells her that he also needs more salsa and avocado, she will groan as she trudges back to aisle 1 again.

When it is time to pay for the groceries, the female and her children will be corralled through passageways filled with candy, soda and trashy magazines. The children will beg for all but the magazines. The female unloads her cart. The items are scanned and bagged. They are loaded into the cart again before being unloaded into the back of the human's car.

Note: The grocery store staff does not follow the female home to help unload the groceries. And often, her children don't help either.

The female will spend about an hour putting away her groceries, throwing out old, spoiled food, and stuffing plastic bags into a tube, to be used later as a sack for dirty diapers. At first her pantry will seem full and satisfying. One day later, however, someone—probably her husband—will open the refrigerator door and say, "Don't we have anything to eat? When are you going to the store?" Soon after, the process begins again.

If this is what an otter child's book about human food would be like, then surely, after the child has read it to his otter mother, she will feel exhausted just for having listened. Then she will say, "That's a lot of work for some food. Now scurry away, son, and find us a good clam. And don't forget the rock."

THE BROTHERS' SEPARATION

SEVEN AND A HALF YEARS AGO, WE BROUGHT HOME A NEW-born baby, Owen, and moved Ford, then just two days past his second birthday, out of his crib and into a toddler bed. Our house was small, so the crib and the toddler bed were in the same room, a mere six feet apart. I worried that Ford might unwittingly harm his new brother while trying to help (placing a blanket over him, throwing a hard plastic Superman into him, etc.), so I bought a netted tent and attached it to the top of Owen's crib. There was a zipper on the side, and that's how we got Owen in and out for naps and bedtime.

Several years later, we bought a second, matching toddler bed for Owen and placed it parallel to Ford's. Owen's quilt had zoo animal prints on it; Ford's was plaid. When Ford started kindergarten, we bought two twin beds (matching, of course) to replace the toddler ones. I got identical sports-themed quilts and sheets for them. The boys shared a dresser, a closet and a bookshelf. They never complained. They never argued. Indeed, they begged us not to ever separate them.

Once, when Ford had learned to read and Owen still had not, we heard the boys talking in their room past bedtime.

"Turn out your lights and get to bed," I yelled from the living room.

"But Ford hasn't finished reading the Bible to me," Owen answered back.

"Oh. Well. Carry on, then."

Owen, who suffered for years from night terrors, often woke with a start in the middle of the night. Through the baby monitor, we sometimes could hear Ford saying, "It's okay, Owen. I'm here. It's me, Ford."

To say that the boys had become codependent is an understatement. They were in a rhythm all their own. Ford's constant humming was background noise for Owen, and Ford learned to sleep with the lights on when Owen was afraid of the dark. Owen picked up Ford's dirty clothes and put them in the hamper; Ford taught Owen how to wear a necktie.

Last Christmas, I bought the boys separate piggy banks because they had always shared one. Ford asked me to return it. "I do all our finances," he said. "So we only need one bank." It was true. Ford counted and stored their respective money, and sometimes, when Owen was short a few dollars for a new toy at the store, Ford would give him extra from his own share.

All of this comes to an end next week. For reasons I don't yet fully understand, I decided that it is time for Ford to have his own room and to move our youngest son, Lindell, 3, into the room with Owen. Ford, who will be 10 years old in November, is (outwardly) thrilled at the opportunity. Owen isn't taking it so well.

Remember how I told you in a previous column that spouses argue before a deployment because it is easier to say goodbye to someone who annoys you? Well, it appears as if Ford and Owen are going through a version of this. For the first time in 7½ years, they are fighting over keeping the lights and the fan on or off overnight. They are bickering about money. And suddenly, Ford's untidy tendencies have begun to grate on Owen's nerves.

Yet, Owen cried himself to sleep one night because of the coming separation. Ford, for all his expressed excitement over having a new room, has mentioned feeling sad about leaving behind his old bed, sheets, quilt and dresser—metaphors, I am sure, for his relationship with Owen.

We counted their money the other day and split it evenly between them. I bought Owen his own bank with a secret combination lock. We've also sorted through and divided their books, neckties and dress socks. The last step before the big switch is to divvy up the *Star Wars* action figures, which have always shared a plastic storage bin underneath the beds. I expect this to be the most difficult part of the divorce, if you will, and won't be surprised if it goes to mediation.

It is the end of an era, and each of the boys is dealing with it in his own, personal way. Much like pre-deployment, Owen is mustering the independence he will need to foster a new, younger roommate (Lindell) in Ford's absence. Now Owen will take care of the finances, and he can read the Bible to Lindell.

I've done my share of crying over the transition, too. It has never not been "Ford and Owen's room." But I'm excited for Lindell and his opportunity to create new, special memories with Owen. And I am comforted by the fact that the bond Ford and Owen built in these past 7 years can withstand any distance, whether it be a hallway, different schools or homes of their own hundreds of miles apart.

FIRSTBORN CUTS PATH

A READER RECENTLY SUGGESTED THAT I MOSTLY, AND UN-fairly, write about my oldest son, Ford, 10. This reader should take a ticket and get in line behind my other children, Owen, 8, and Lindell, 3, to file his grievance.

Owen and Lindell are more likely to complain about who gets more cookies or a bigger present than what I write about. Still, I have limited patience for the whole fairness thing. Therefore, the file-your-grievances-here line moves rather slowly. In fact, with multiple children, the line is a lot like my e-mail inbox—it's never empty.

Of course, this reader's comment is nothing new. Several times a year, in response to various columns, readers write to tell me that I favor Ford. This is a relief to Dustin because it means that people have forgotten all the columns about him. I remind these readers that I do write about Lindell and that Owen, after the whole waffle-flopper incident, requested that I never put his name in print again. He has since retracted his request, but I'm still gun-shy.

There is some truth to these readers' accusations. Col-umns about Ford are second in number only to columns about Dustin having another, well, moment. But this doesn't mean that I favor Ford more than I favor my other children. It means that his experiences are more novel and interesting.

Here's why:

Ford, like all firstborn children, is a human weed whacker. He is walking through the dense woods of growing up, and overgrown limbs (learning experiences) and weeds (life lessons) are smacking him in the face. He can't see far in front of him because there are only more and more weeds and limbs. He knows these will also whip him in the face as he passes by, clearing a path.

Owen, like all second-born children, is crouched behind Ford and grimacing every time he hears a limb snap or his older brother moan in agony. His hands are on Ford's waist, and he leans his body this way and that, daring to look, then retreating to the safety of Ford's back. But mostly, Owen is thankful for a cleared walkway. He has never had to weed-whack. Ford's face is marked by all the obstacles he has forced out of the way; Owen's face has seldom met a twig that didn't hit his brother's face first.

You can see this when they are getting ready for school in the morning. While I am scolding Ford for losing his gloves and hat (again), Owen slinks away to find his own. Soon he is completely dressed and waiting on the front porch, undoubtedly making mental notes about where to keep his winter gear in the future so that he will never lose them.

You also can see it when Ford comes home from school with new information about what is and is not cool. Ford has to learn these things as they hit him in the face. Not only does Owen have the benefit of advance notice, but his path has been cleared, too.

Lindell is so far removed from the weed whacker, he is simply drafting. He does not know that there ever were limbs and weeds. Sometimes this is to his detriment. The path, un-expectedly, has regrown partially in between him and Owen. This is what makes Lindell more like Ford than Owen.

But there is another side to this. As Ford is clearing the way, his experiences are new for me, too. Parents talk about this a lot, only in different language: the diminishing scrap-books and birthday extravaganzas. These are mere symptoms of a larger issue. It's not that the second and third children are less loved, it's that the experiences of the second and third are less dramatic (less snapping, less scarring, less weed whacking) and therefore less notable.

I cried the whole week before Ford turned 10 years old. I wrote a column about it, too. In two years, when Owen turns 10, or in 7 years when Lindell does, the experience will not be as brutal. I may or may not feel compelled to write a column about it.

Of course, there also are life's little surprises, things that don't follow the order of first, second and third. I know that Ford's first word was dog (spoken as "God"), and Owen's first word was probably "car" (spoken like a Mainer: "cah"), but even though Lindell is last, and theoretically his first word should be somewhat less memorable, I know, because it devastated me so much, that his was "SpongeBob." He had veered from the path. In fact, it could be argued that Ford and Owen had led him there.

Which leads me to wonder, where were the park rangers when all this SpongeBob-watching was happening? Most likely, they were tired.

Loss of Wii: Cruel and Unusual Punishment

My family had become obsessed with Wii. I was the last holdout, having already completed Super Mario Bros. when I was 12 years old. Then, in an impulsive moment, I purchased the game Tetris at a local toy store. No one was safe anymore.

Granted, I did not stoop as low as my young children, who were literally pounding each other on the ground to defend their Wii mastery, but I came close when I called Dustin a "loser" for standing between me and the television screen.

Our family was becoming unglued. Worse, we weren't getting much done. It all came to an end last Saturday.

I was cooking dinner downstairs, and the noise that erupted one floor above me, where Lindell and Owen were playing Wii, sounded like two cats fighting in the bushes. Lindell was crying like someone had stolen his dinner. Owen was screaming "Liiiinnndeeellll" in the familiar warning-shot tone that means a fight is about to happen. I knew they were on the ground wrestling when the chandelier above the kitchen table shook back and forth and rattled.

What I'm about to describe next is a well-intended parenting tactic gone horribly wrong. I remembered my friend Steph telling me earlier in the day that she had "done away" (wink, wink) with her family's Wii, and that they had been searching for it ever since. It sounded like such a peaceful resolution.

Before I had time to think it through, however, I was running up the stairs two steps at a time. My heart was beating in my throat. I stepped over the pile of boys rolling across the floor, grabbed the Wii modem and literally yanked it out of the wall. The wires left behind hung from the cabinet like the roots of a dug-up plant. The television screen went black. I don't think the Wii made a noise when it lost power, so that thud I recall must have been my children's hearts skipping a beat.

I ran to my bedroom with the Wii tucked under my arm like a football. Then I threw (not "placed") the modem into my closet and shut the door. When I walked back out, the boys were frozen with disbelief. I went downstairs without saying a word.

Before I got to the kitchen, the crying and moaning began. (News flash: The world technically ended last Saturday.) You would have thought I had given away the family pet. Or thrown away the rest of the Halloween candy. The boys' reaction only solidified my decision, even as I knew that I had not gone about it in the peaceful way that Steph had.

Dustin came home in the middle of this. Which is to say, he unknowingly walked into World War III. Kids were screaming and kicking walls in their bedrooms. Dinner was boiling over on the kitchen stove. I was sitting at the table with my head in my hands. It only could have been more startling if I had been clutching one of the lifeless chords to my chest.

"I did a bad thing," I said.

Dustin looked scared.

"I unhooked the Wii."

"Oh, well, good for you," Dustin said. "It's about time our family got rid of that thing."

Owen came out of his room. "But Dad, she made us lose all of our progress! We will have to do all those worlds again."

Now Dustin looked like he might cry and kick walls, too. He struggled to get his "Man of the House" face back in order.

"I don't believe that will be the case," Dustin told Owen. "I think our progress will be saved. And if it isn't, we will get there again. But, ahem, well, I support your mother and her decision. This is good for us . . . I mean, you."

That night, Dustin, who is reading all the classics to the children for bedtime stories, read a chapter of *Frankenstein* aloud to Owen and Lindell. I overheard him as I cleaned dishes in the next room. Although this version of *Frankenstein* is part of the Great Illustrated Classics series and therefore not as intense as the original, it still has some gruesome ideas and descriptions. I was surprised that no one was crying and saying they were scared. Indeed, both of them were riveted.

When Dustin was finished and came back into the kitchen, I asked him, "Do you think that book is a little much for them?"

"Have you ever read *Frankenstein*?" He asked. "It has a great message. And it's a classic." (They had just finished reading *Dr. Jekyll and Mr. Hyde* the week before.)

Dustin went to the living room to watch football. I dried the dishes and considered all that had happened, how I had run up the stairs like a monster and pulled the Wii from its life source. How the kids had screamed and cried like their dog had died. How the dinner had almost caught fire on the stove. And I realized that of course the kids can handle *Frankenstein*. After losing their Wii, nothing could ever really be scary again.

ETCHINGS ON THE FAMILY TABLE

WHEN I WAS GROWING UP, MY FAMILY ATE DINNER TOgether at an old wooden farm table. The nightly tradition was formal, in that we were expected to use manners and not sit on our feet, but mostly it was relaxed and without any extraneous rules. Certainly there were no assigned seats. Even so, for 20 years, my two older brothers, Van and Will, my parents and I sat at the same spots, as if they were given to us, around the table.

I sat next to Will (but still far enough away that he was once able to hurl a biscuit at me) and across from my mom, who was to the left of Van. Dad, when he was not on deployment, sat to my right, at the head of the table. Although this seating arrangement originated at the family dinner table, it became so comfortable that we still unknowingly fall into our usual spots, even when we are at a restaurant.

Because the dinner table was at the center of the kitchen, which was the hub of the house, we often used it for other tasks not related to mealtimes. I rolled out Play-Doh there, baked cookies in my Easy-Bake oven, did homework, made birthday cards for friends, wrapped presents and played board games. In doing so, my brothers and I over the years had accidentally carved a timeline of our childhoods into the soft wood of the table at each of our respective spots.

At my place you could see the word "COKE" dug into the grain because I hadn't put enough paper underneath when I pretended to be a waitress taking orders. At Will's place there were dented spirals made into flowers from his experiment with a Spirograph. All over the table, when the sunlight hit it just right, you could see jumbled words dug into the wood from where we had done our homework.

Now that my original family has grown by three spouses and four grandchildren, Mom replaced the old dinner table with a longer (but still old) farm table. It took a while for Dustin to realize that no matter how many people show up at my parents' house, Mom will fit them around the dinner table. You don't sit in front of the television with your meal in your lap at Mom's house. You don't go out to eat that often either. You squeeze into your spot at the table, where there will be a place mat and silverware waiting for you.

When Mom upgraded her table, she gave the old one to me. Dad spent several hours sanding the soft wood, years of accidental carvings turning into sawdust and blowing into the wind, so that he could put a new coat of varnish on top. When he was finished, the table shone like it never had before. The wood was smooth and without any blemishes. Even my "COKE" was erased. It was like a fresh sheet of paper—an unmarked canvas—for my family of five to create our own dinnertime memories upon.

Except, I didn't want my boys to mark up the "new" shiny table. "Get something to bear down on," I told them hundreds of times a day as they sat down to draw or do homework. Eventually, however, the table began to show the etchings of our lives: the words of Ford's thank-you note to a friend; numbers from Owen's schoolwork; dots like acne scars where Lindell bangs his fork; the discolored circle where I set down a hot pan.

I've noticed that as the boys get older, they spend less time at the kitchen table with coloring books and toys, and a family dinnertime has become even more important. But the boys often are busy—too busy—with after-school sports and activities. Every night we have a different commitment to meet, a practice to get to, a meeting to attend. Last week, our schedules were so packed we didn't sit down together once for dinner. So I pulled the plug on some activities and asked the boys to choose one sport for each season. I told them that our family will eat together at least three times a week, even at the sacrifice of after-school events.

Many people will disagree with me. There is much to learn and pack into a childhood, after all, and denying a child the opportunity to participate in several activities almost seems unfair.

But recently it occurred to me that there are worse things than asking your child to pick only one extracurricular commitment at a time. For instance, raising children to adulthood with a kitchen table that never receives a scratch or a dent, those tattoos of a family sitting together for a meal, and missing out on the irreplaceable memories that go with them.

Price Gouging Gumballs

Gumballs, increasingly in low supply here at the Smiley house, have become a hot commodity. Of course, no one cared about gumballs, a box of which had been on the boys' dresser since Christmas, until last week. In fact, last month I vacuumed up a few that had fallen between a bed and the wall, and no one noticed. Now you can earn a good $10 if you stumble across one.

I first became aware of the black market for gumballs when I was sitting at the kitchen table, minding my own business, and through the wall behind me, I heard a fight break out in Lindell and Owen's room.

"Those are not your balls" is a really awkward thing to hear your kids yell at one another.

I should mention how I know that the boys are fighting by sound alone. Basically, the walls shake until the decorative plates hanging in our kitchen rattle and swing on their hooks. When things get really bad, I can hear what sounds like a baseball bat, but is probably someone's elbow or knee, hitting the floor. Mostly however, there is the usual sound of a tussle: toys crashing, feet pounding and the occasional, "I said, 'Give it back!'" or "I'm telling!"

For the most part, I believe in letting the boys work things out themselves. Also, because I grew up with two older brothers, I know that boys' play (even their "fighting") sounds worse than it is, and that males have a certain amount of physical aggression they need to let out. But there are times when I catch myself wondering, "Will they actually seriously hurt each other?" That's when I go into the room and pull them off one another.

On this particular day, when I separated the boys, I noticed that Lindell was clutching a handful of gumballs that had partially melted and colored his hands red, blue and orange. All three of the boys started talking at once.

"Those are my gumballs and he stole them!"

"He's already lost all his own gumballs [no, they're probably in the vacuum, I thought], so now he's taking mine."

Lindell stuffed several gumballs into his mouth and began to chew.

"Give them back! Give them back!"

And then the highly awkward, "You're not supposed to take my bal- . . . I mean, gum!"

"Fine, you owe me one dollar," Ford said.

Lindell went to his piggy bank, retrieved a dollar and handed it to Ford. I went back to my seat at the kitchen table. Sure, I felt bad that my 4-year-old was gypped by his older brother, but there are worse things (such as sitting through economics class) than overpaying for gumballs. Consider it an interesting lesson in supply and demand.

A few minutes later, I heard Lindell say, "I want to buy another gumball."

"That will be one dollar," Ford said.

This went on for several more times. Then Ford came out of his room with a shocking announcement: "We are almost out of gumballs."

Lindell raced to his piggy bank again.

"So I've raised the price to $10 per ball," Ford said.

Lindell stopped. He didn't have $10.

"I'd like to cut you a deal," Ford said. "But in these hard times of so few gumballs, I can't really afford to."

The market finally had crashed. I went back to my business. The house was quiet again. Then suddenly the plates began to rattle.

"Lindell is stealing my gumballs," Ford yelled.

Lindell ran past me with a mouth full of gum and colored goo dripping from the corner of his lips.

"You are in debt now, Lindell," Ford said, chasing after him. "You owe the bank [apparently, that's Ford] more money than you can possible earn in a year. This is serious!"

However, by the look on Lindell's face—his cheeks full like a chipmunk—it was obvious that he was not really concerned about his financial problems. Later, when Lindell realized his predicament, he tried to sell back some gum. But the market already had tanked.

Eventually I asked Ford, "How much money did you make off your brother?"

"About $15."

That's a lot of gum! So I asked Lindell where he was keeping all this gum, or, more precisely, where he was putting it when he was done chewing it.

He said, "I've eaten a few, swallowed some, left one in the bathroom and I have a couple in my pocket."

(Someday he'll learn that he should have hidden those gumballs and resold them when the market rose again.)

After Valentine's Day, Ford realized that between their grandparents' cards, each of the boys had received $30. He told Lindell: "You can buy three gumballs now."

Lindell, who was sitting in his car seat and sucking on a lollipop, did not hesitate when he said: "Nope. Because I got this lollipop for free."

PICTURE FRAMES AS TIME CAPSULES

ON THE TABLE NEXT TO OUR FRONT DOOR IS A 4-BY-6 INCH frame that holds a picture of Lindell, 11 months old, sitting for the first time on the beach in Pensacola, Fla. He is holding up his right hand to inspect the white grains of sand between his pudgy fingers.

This image is hardly representative of Lindell now. He's more likely to moon me on the beach than sit for a posed photograph. Still, I keep the picture, in that particular frame, where it will stay for many years to come.

If you open the back of the frame—indeed, if you open the back of any frame in my house—a stack of older photographs will spill out. Even as I replace images by covering them up with newer ones, I almost never remove them entirely. I cannot bear to.

Behind the picture of Lindell on the beach are probably six or seven other pictures: of Owen as a baby, then Ford as a baby, and maybe even one from our wedding day. In this way, decorative frames are Smiley family time capsules.

Of course, this result has been mostly unexpected and unintended. Pictures stack up behind newer pictures because I do not have the emotional strength to remove them. (What do you do with a photograph you once treasured enough to frame? Do you put it in a shoebox with all the other photographs, the ones you didn't think to frame before?)

On a wall across from the picture of Lindell is a long, vertical frame with three openings. Since 2005, it has show-cased portraits of Ford, then 4, and Owen, then 2. One day I walked past and noticed the pictures, but I hardly recognized the children in them. Owen's long, slender nose was still undefined, and his cheeks were full of baby fat. Ford's front teeth—still not the adult ones—were small, almost forgettable compared with his big brown eyes and head. He had chubby cheeks, too.

I stared at those pictures for a long time, my reflection in the glass casting a shadow over their baby faces. My face, with its lines and shape, was still the same. But these children! Well, I had to think hard to remember how they were. What were their voices like? How did they laugh? What did their hands feel like in mine?

I know that parents dread the day their children leave home. And I know parents grieve during the first few years of an empty nest. Yet I've found that through all the years beforehand, children are leaving their parents one impercep-tible moment at a time. There is constant grieving.

My 4-year-old Owen, that timid toddler whose hair al-ways stuck up, lives only in my memory and old photographs now. He's been replaced by a talkative boy with a sharp nose and a keen sense of humor. And the way that the padding of Lindell's diaper felt when he was sitting on my hip in his denim overalls—it too vanishes from mind like a dream you can just barely remember after you've woken up.

All those moments are stored in the backs of picture frames, one after the other, safe behind a plate of glass.

But in that vertical frame with three openings, there has never been a picture of Lindell. I knew this needed attention. So I hired a photographer to take pictures of the boys, and I ordered one of each of them to fill the frame.

The day the prints arrived, I took the frame off the wall, turned it over on the kitchen table and unfastened the backing. Unlike other frames that are suitable for storing past photos, this frame, because of its design, would not. The old pictures of Ford and Owen were fastened to the matte with tape. They would have to come out and be stored elsewhere.

With the matte and images facedown, I could see the silhouette of my babies' faces through the backside of the paper. With each tender tug of the tape, I second-guessed my decision. Was I ready to have those smiles stored away?

Once I had safely removed the photographs, I looked up and realized that the 4-year-old picture of Ford and 10-year-old picture of Ford were side-by-side on the table. It took me a few moments to get past that. Then I carried the old pictures of Ford and Owen upstairs and searched for a place to store them. I decided to put them in the back of another frame.

Eventually, I had three new photographs mounted in the frame. I hung it on the wall and was pleased. The fame very much represents my life today: Ford, Owen and Lindell. My three boys, as I know them now, are smiling at me when I walk in the front door.

Except, someday, even those photographs will seem old, the images young and hard to remember.

I dread that.

First Fish, Then Dog

LINDELL DESPERATELY WANTS A DOG, SO LAST WEEK WE bought him a fish. He's still too young to realize this doesn't add up. And anyway, the excitement of a new pet—any kind of pet—is enough.

At the pet store, however, we met several obstacles.

"You have to cycle the tank first," the fish expert told us. "The water has to build bacteria for a week before you can put a fish in it."

"But I promised my son a fish today."

"Then I guess this is a good time to teach him patience."

I must have looked like a lunatic mother. In fact, I hadn't had a chance to comb my hair that morning and I was wearing the same clothes from the day before.

"I've been trying to teach him that for four years!" I said.

The clean-cut, 20-something boy looked scared. He backed away from me and glanced over his left and right shoulders. "Might I suggest a betta fish," he said.

A betta-what?

Apparently betta fish can come to the surface and breathe oxygen, so high levels of ammonia and nitrites do not put them at risk during the tank's initial "startup cycle." But betta fish are kind of sleepy and boring looking. They live in plastic containers the size of a tub of butter. They have nothing on the see-through glass catfish or the the minia-ture shark fish my kids were eyeing.

So we bought a pink betta and decided it would be mine. In other words, I took one for the team. In a week, once the pH levels in the water have settled, the boys, and in particular Lindell, could pick out something cool like a bumblebee fish.

"Now you need a heater, filter, substrate and perhaps some live plants," the expert said. All to keep the water in balance, of course.

I was beginning to think a dog might have been easier. Then I remembered the border collie we used to own. She once dug up a small tree in our front yard and ran down the street with it clenched between her teeth. Sometimes sleepy is good.

"Maybe we could get two betta fish," one of the boys suggested.

That's when the expert told us that multiple betta fish will attack and kill each other. Note: Do not tell three boys that two incompatible fish will fight each other if your intent is to *decrease* their enthusiasm.

The five of us spent the next two hours at home setting up our new aquarium. Here are a few things I learned:

- Position the tank first; fill it with water second.
- Ten gallons is a lot of water to spill on the floor.
- A 4-year-old can't carry a pitcher full of water.
- Betta fish get lively when they are out of the tub-of-butter container.

Next, Lindell named the betta fish, which was really my fish, but which I lent to Lindell until he can get a different fish. He named her Puffy Fluffy.

One by one, the boys carefully placed the ornaments they had selected for the aquarium into the substrate (fancy name for rocks). Ford's was a piece of driftwood with a live plant growing on it. Owen's was a tiki head that for some reason caused the children to erupt into a song: hoo, haa, hee, tiki, tiki. And the last ornament was Lindell's: a bright yellow pineapple house and a tiny SpongeBob SquarePants figurine (it was like watching a touchdown in the Super Bowl when Puffy Fluffy finally, days later, swam through the holes of the pineapple house).

Everyone dreamed about what kind of fish they would get in a week. Ford wanted a glass catfish. Owen liked the lionfish but, unfortunately, it is suitable only for salt water. Lindell wanted the mysterious "skeleton fish" that no one else had actually seen at the pet store. I saw more tears in my future.

"I guess I'll get a bottom feeder," Dustin said. "Because someone has to."

Dustin, taking the next one for the team. I wonder whether he will let Lindell name his fish, too. And I wonder whether Lindell will name it something like "Dave." If he names it "Skinny Minny," I might be offended.

That first night, all three boys fell asleep watching the fish tank. After we carried them to their beds, Dustin and I watched it, too. I remembered the fullness of having a family pet. Even if it is a fish. And then I remembered the heartache of watching our past pets leave us. I wondered, why do we set ourselves up like this. Why do we bring animals into our lives when we know someday we will have to say good-bye or, um, flush them down the toilet?

Well, I decided that we do it because a boy needs a dog—to take to camp, to chase in the backyard, to sleep at the foot of his bed. And according to Dad, the boy has to start with a fish. We are off to a good start.

WE WON A SHARK

IT HAS BECOME A SUMMER TRADITION TO TAKE MY BOYS TO the city fair and then regret it afterward. I leave feeling like I need to take a bath in hand sanitizer, and I want those three hours of my life back. Yet, no trip to the fair has been more regrettable than this year's. That's when we bought—I mean, won—a shark. Wait, did I say shark? I meant fish.

Lindell's and Owen's Ping-Pong balls had landed in a bowl filled with colored water, so the carnival worker told us they had won fish. This, I thought, was at least better than winning a stuffed banana—which we had done previously. After all, we needed new fish because four in our tank had died. The only two left were my betta fish, Aqua, and Dustin's bottom feeder, Barnacle Boy.

The mustached carnival worker handed Lindell and Owen plastic bags filled with water and one lone fish swimming at the bottom.

"Will these be okay with our betta fish at home?" I said, because I know that betta fish often don't like to share space. "Will our betta fish hurt them?"

The carnival man smiled. "I wouldn't worry about these fish," he said. (In storytelling, this is what we call foreshadowing. In movies, this is where the music gets creepy.)

Owen named his fish Frisky. Lindell named his Fred. One week later, however, Fred's name, in light of recent events, was changed to Fred the Killer Fish.

Frisky and Fred were excited when we dumped them into the tank. They flitted around the "No Fishing" sign and in and out of the SpongeBob SquarePants pineapple house. As usual, Aqua kept her distance. Barnacle Boy hid under the tikki. As far as we could tell, they were a tolerable, if cautious, new family of four.

Then, a few days later, Owen came out of his room and solemnly said, "Mom, a fish has died."

Ford was close behind him: "Mom, a fish didn't just die; there was a massacre in the tank."

"Oh, stop being dramatic," I said. I set the newspaper on the kitchen table and got up to take a look.

When I rounded the corner and came within full view of the tank, here's what I saw: Frisky caught in the upward bubbles of the filter, bobbing up and down, with his tail fin chewed completely off and one eyeball gone. Bits of skin trailed from him like streamers.

I gasped. Lindell cried, "Mommy, I'm scared."

I patted Lindell's head as the words of the man at the carnival echoed in my mind: "I wouldn't worry about these fish."

We flushed Frisky and scolded Aqua. Wow, betta fish really are aggressive, we said. We should have known that Aqua wouldn't accept the new, innocent carnie fish.

One week later, terror struck again.

"Mom, Aqua is dead!" Lindell screamed.

"It's another massacre," Ford said. They were both running from the room.

I sprinted to the tank, my sock-feet sliding across the wood floor as I came to a stop. Aqua's head was half buried beneath the gravel rocks. Parts of her skin had been peeled away. You could see the bones in her head.

My cheeks turned cold. "Boys, we have a killer fish on our hands," I said.

Lindell began to cry.

"We have to kill him before he kills us," Ford said.

"What? Did they give us, a shark?" Owen asked.

Silently, I regretted blaming Aqua for Frisky's death. In the tank, Fred glided from one end of the tank to the other. He was deliberate and emotionless. I knew the scene looked bad, but still, someone had to stay open-minded. I mean, Fred was from the carnival, but that didn't necessarily make him a murderer.

"How do we know it isn't Barnacle Boy who is killing everyone?" I asked.

"Mom, look at Barnacle Boy," Ford said. "He eats algae and sucks on the side of the glass. He didn't murder anyone."

It's true. Barnacle Boy hardly looks like a menace with his open-mouthed fish-face stuck to the side of the tank.

Ford looked at me seriously. "Mom, we have to kill Fred," he said.

"No!" I bristled at the idea, even as I secretly considered locking the aquarium in the basement—just in case. "I'm not killing a possibly innocent fish. Either Barnacle Boy and Fred will live peacefully together, or we will eventually know who the real killer is."

We have daily "tank watches" now. Some of us think Fred is growing bigger by the minute. Others think Barnacle Boy is not what he seems. When I told the boys that one day, while I had the tank cover open to feed the fish, I heard Barnacle Boy say, "You're not going to leave me in here with that carnie, are you?" they believed me.

In hindsight, when I asked the carnival man, "Will these fish be okay with our betta at home?" apparently I had asked the wrong question. I'm frightened for anyone who won a "stuffed" clown or baby doll. Lock those things in the basement, please.

Fred is still living. So is Barnacle Boy. For now. Occasionally Lindell comes into my room at night because he's afraid of Fred. I open the covers and let him in, because, quite frankly, I don't blame him.

MEET SPARKY

MY YOUNGEST SON, LINDELL, 4, HAS HAD JUST ONE ASPIRA-tion: to be a dog. I'm not joking. And neither is he.

Before Lindell knew his ABCs, he was fetching a tennis ball . . . with his mouth.

Oh, I had tried to stop this behavior, and I put my foot down when he asked to be fed from a bowl on the floor. But soon it became obvious that Lindell really does have a deep affinity for animals, specifically dogs. We bought him stuffed animals and even live fish (Note: a fish is a not a dog). These only satisfied Lindell temporarily.

Then Lindell started asking us to refer to him as Scooby. He pawed at my thighs while I was washing dishes, and he licked Dustin's face. When he called me Daphne in the middle of Kohl's, and I replied reflexively, "Yes, Scoob," on-lookers stifled their laughs.

Sometimes Lindell switched and asked us to call him Sparky. Eventually, however, Sparky became the name Lin-dell said he would name his own dog, the one he was sure he would get some day soon.

"Not now," Dustin said. "There's no chance we're getting a dog."

"Are you sure, Dustin?" I said after Lindell went to bed. "Think about how excited the kids would be."

"No. Not a chance. It's not the right time."

That was early October. Slowly, I began pressing Dustin:

"Maybe a dog would help Lindell overcome his habit of fetching tennis balls. Maybe he'd stop asking for Scooby Snacks. And his older brothers are always busy doing other things; a dog would be a playmate for Lindell. I'd take care of it, of course. You wouldn't be responsible for anything. I'd even clean up all the, um, you know."

"No. Not a chance. We've already talked about this."

A week later, Dustin went to the Humane Society after work to pick out a dog for me. The one he had his eye on had already been adopted. When Dustin came home and told me this, I secretly marveled at my powers, powers I'd like to harness. How did I bring him from "no" to "how soon can we get a dog?" in the course of one week? Because there are plenty of other things I want, too.

By the week of Halloween, we had found another dog. We didn't tell the kids. In fact, as late as the day before we got our new dog, I told the boys again, "Stop asking for a dog! It will be a while before we can get a dog!"

And then, 24 hours later, we surprised them after school.

I believe there are moments in our life we never forget, snapshots stored away in our permanent memory. The look on Lindell's face when he first saw Sparky is, for me, one of those moments.

That first night, Sparky got a taste of his new life: constantly being petted, chased, followed, tugged and stalked by a little boy in a Scooby Doo costume. The two dogs even took a nap together on Sparky's pillow.

Then a funny thing happened, something only Dustin claims to have predicted. Lindell became jealous of the dog. He wanted his own leash and collar. He wanted his own crate. He was sad that everyone pet Sparky more than they pet him.

We had tapped into a new realm of sibling rivalry. And after a quick search on Amazon.com, there isn't even a self-help book for dealing with this.

Maybe we are the only ones with a son who thinks he's a dog and is jealous of his family's real dog.

"I think Lindell is just now realizing he's not actually a dog," Dustin said.

But sometimes, struggling is a good thing. Every first-born child is made stronger and more tolerant by the arrival of a new sibling. And so it will be with Lindell and Sparky. Already, they are easing into their new roles.

Sparky is accepting his doghood, and Lindell is accepting his humanness.

And all the while, a new friendship is forming between the two species.

Sparky is the first thing Lindell looks for when he wakes up in the morning. And Sparky never misses a chance to sniff Lindell's grubby pants and hands. He is fond of grabbing Scooby's stuffed costume tail and following him around the house that way. Lindell is barking less, no longer chasing his "tail" and responding to "Lindell" more. If we never could get him trained, it looks like Sparky might.

A week later, I was petting Sparky on the living room floor and said over my shoulder to Dustin, "So, what changed your mind about getting a dog? How did I convince you in just a week?"

Dustin hesitated, reluctant to give me insight into my powers. Because that would be like letting a dog see from which pocket he gets his treats.

I turned around to look at Dustin. "Seriously, why did you decide to get me and the kids a dog?"

Dustin smiled and reached out to pet Sparky. "Because you only live once," he said.

Yes, I think even Dustin has found a best friend in Sparky.

WHEN A DOG TRAINS HIS BOY

MANY PEOPLE WERE SHOCKED WHEN DUSTIN AND I SUR-
prised the boys last Halloween with a puppy, just three
weeks before Dustin left for his deployment.

"Are you sure you want to take on the extra responsibil-
ity?" they asked.

And, "Do you know what you're getting into?"

What most people didn't know, however, was that we
had a 4-year-old who believed he was a dog, to the point of
eating off the floor and carrying a tennis ball in his mouth.

Before Sparky, the last dog we lived with was a border
collie named Annie, who, I suspect, could manage pre-algebra.
She was one of the smartest dogs I've ever known, except for
that time she ate an SOS steel wool pad.

But Annie also liked to eat wood—specifically, our back
porch—so she left us to work on a 13-acre farm in Florida.

Lindell never knew Annie.

We had a long, pet-free period (unless you count fish),
until one year ago when the boys ran from the schoolyard to
greet the new puppy waiting for them on the sidewalk. So
long as Sparky wasn't on a mission, like Annie, to destroy every
single thing we own, I knew he would be a welcome addition.

Yes, even though Dustin was leaving.

You see, as it turns out, Sparky, a Brittany spaniel, has
been a great distraction, especially for Lindell. Sparky has

been cried on, hugged (perhaps too tightly) and fought over ("He's sleeping in my room." "No, my room!").

Sparky even was an accomplice to the great "runaway episode" several months ago. I can't say which one, but a son ran away to the end of the street with no suitcase or change of clothes, but with a willing dog, who likes to go on walks, by his side.

Sparky has also done wonders for Lindell's confusion about being a dog.

At first, Sparky and Lindell had some "getting used to" (Lindell's words) to do. Sparky often sighed, and sometimes ran away, when Lindell came near. This might have had something to do with the Scooby-Doo costume Lindell wore and the fact that he took naps in Sparky's bed—usually on top of Sparky.

Eventually, however, Lindell "learned Sparky's lessons" (again, Lindell's words), and besides that time Sparky ran out the backdoor with Lindell's underwear, the two seldom make each other cry. They have settled into a nice, passive-aggressive relationship of sibling rivalry.

Sparky has brought out many aspects of all my boys' personalities. Lindell is the instigator. He is not opposed to blaming his mess on Sparky. Ford is the dutiful helper, always willing to take Sparky for a walk or feed him break-fast. Owen is the empathizer. When Sparky had to wear the dreaded "cone of shame" (a post-surgery e-collar) last week, Owen hand-fed his meals to him.

Just as a husband and wife unite in their children, the older boys and I have bonded over our shared love of

Sparky. When we pick up Sparky after a bath or time spent playing with another dog, Ford and Owen smile uncontrollably.

"Look at him just sitting there with those other dogs," they say. Or, "Look at how smart he is."

This reminds me of parents' behavior when they pick up their children at school. Also, it reminds me of the way Ford and Owen act when they see Lindell playing at the park with friends.

Lindell doesn't participate in these loving observations of Sparky, because he doesn't view Sparky as a "child." He sees him as a brother. While Lindell has moved past believing he himself is 100 percent dog (it's been a long time since he carried a tennis ball in his mouth), he and Sparky are still, in many ways, growing up together. They are in parallel states of innocence and wonder.

I wish I could suspend them there.

Soon, Lindell will move past Sparky (age- and experience-wise), even though I know he will never outgrow him. There will always be a little piece of Lindell that is part-Sparky/dog.

Which brings me back to Lindell's species identity.

When my mother-in-law, Robin, was visiting last month, she told the boys about a new way to study genealogy. Using a test-tube provided by a scientific company, Robin sends a sample of her saliva to be analyzed for DNA. The results tell her what percentage of her DNA is European, Middle Eastern, etc.

Ford's and Owen's eyes lit up at the thought.

Later, they asked me, "Can we do this with Lindell and add a little bit of Sparky's spit before sending it off, so that the results come back with 'You are 10 percent dog?'"

I laughed. And then I felt sad. If that could actually work—if it would keep my two youngest boys, Lindell and Sparky, in a suspended state of blissful innocence—I just might try it.

TO THE LITTLEST BOY IN STRIPED SHIRTS

To the Littlest Boy in Striped Shirts,

I knew from the first time you spilled apple juice in your lap at the kitchen table that we were going to be great friends. These other people, the bigger ones, they never spill. They eat all their food, and usually right in front of me. They sit on the couch and eat that turkey sandwich one delicious bite at a time. And I watch. Oh, yeah, I watch.

But you, buddy, you always leave something for me. You walk around with your sandwich held real close—precariously close, some might say—to the ground. The turkey slides out of the bread, and sometimes you leave a trail. I like to think you do this on purpose. And, yes, in case you're wondering, when I snatch the sandwich out of your hand, I'm doing that on purpose, too.

I wasn't sure when I first got here, though. You were even smaller then. You slept in my bed and put my tennis ball in your mouth. Your mom didn't like that very much. Neither did I. I wasn't sure if you were a puppy or I was small human. Then I followed you onto the couch and that cleared things up: No one with fur is allowed on the furniture. You don't have fur, that is obvious, but have these people making the rules seen your sticky hands?

You liked to line me up with stuffed animals—the same ones I'd try to eat later (Note to self: The stuffed bird is off-limits. Chewing him will end with me in my cage in the basement)—and you read stories to us. You read made-up words that weren't on the page, but it didn't matter. All I heard was "turkey sandwich, turkey sandwich" anyway.

In the backyard, you thought I could play soccer and baseball. You cheered every time I accidentally took the ball to the side fence. Yeah, I figured this out. Sadly, I would have done so much more for just a little bit more turkey.

While everyone else makes me "sit," "stay" or "shake" for a treat, you gave me bones just for showing up. When you called my name, it wasn't because you wanted to know where I was. You actually wanted to talk to me. To play with me. And that's why I came running.

But you are growing now, Littlest Boy. Your pants don't smell so bad. (OK, I mean "good." Your pants actually smelled good to me back then.) But you still slip turkey underneath the kitchen table. For that alone, I will follow you to the ends of the Earth. Or, at least the driveway.

Those bigger boys are growing, too, and it worries me. Littlest Boy in Striped Shirts, will you someday shut your bedroom door, too? Will you step over me while you talk on the phone with your friends? Will you eat everything on your plate, ask for more, and not notice me staring up at you?

Although, I must say that I have the oldest one trained well. I ring the bells hanging on the back door, and he lets me out. It doesn't matter if he's upstairs, in the basement or on the phone. He would probably come out of the shower to open the door for me. I ring the bells, he comes running. Fascinating!

But Littlest Boy in Striped Shirts, I think he gets paid for this.

You are gone more often now, and I am home alone. I peruse your bedroom—you know, just in case you left some bite-sized Legos or puzzle pieces on the floor there. I see your stuffed bird taunting me from the top bookshelf, and I smell everything that is you. Sometimes, I nap in your room. I dream about when you used to read to me. If I jerk my legs in my sleep, that's when I'm running with you, the Littlest Boy in Striped Shirts, in the backyard.

Then, when I hear you coming home (I can hear you a mile away, kid—I think everyone can), I run to the steps and wait. Your backpack holds all the smells of your adventure: books, pencils, snack time, dirty tennis shoes and friends who also have sticky hands.

You are busy in the afternoons now. You have sports to play and friends' houses to go to. I spend a lot of time watching out the front window for you. I miss your sandwiches, but I also miss you.

And that is why my favorite part of the day is bedtime. You wait until I'm in my spot next to your bed, and then you read aloud a bedtime story. You check often to make sure I'm still there, guarding you as your eyes start to close.

Don't worry Littlest Boy in Striped Shirts. I am here. And I will be here as long as you will have me.

SAM'S CLUB

MY CHILDREN LEISURELY EAT POPCORN WHILE THEY WATCH Obi-Wan Kenobi defeat Anakin Skywalker in the battle of Mustafar. They laugh with their dad at Saturday Night Live's "Massive Head Wound Harry." They keep action figures and plastic dinosaurs that are missing various body parts. We have a life-size, talking Darth Vader in our basement. Dustin once read *Frankenstein* to the boys as a bedtime story.

So you would think my three boys, ages 5-11, could handle most anything. But I have found their Achilles tendon, the Kryptonite, if you will, for the Smiley boys. Turns out, Ford, Owen and Lindell can't handle Sam's Club.

Why didn't I see this coming? My kids are infamous for bad behavior at a regular grocery store. Sam's Club is like Food Lion on steroids. I should have been prepared.

But I didn't even consider Sam's Club as a shopping option until recently. Why it took me 35 years to find a warehouse full of food, I cannot say. Having my third son should have been an obvious prompt for other people more in the know to suggest the idea of bulk-food shopping to me. There I was buying soup can-by-can at the local grocery store when I could have been buying a whole flat of it.

Thankfully, I was finally made aware of these missed opportunities when a friend mentioned that I could buy Goldfish crackers by the pound at Sam's Club.

She didn't have to tell me twice.

On the way to Sam's, I prepared the children for what they might experience. "This will be like nothing you've ever seen before," I said. "There will be food from floor to ceiling. And Sam's Club might sell other things like televisions, underwear and books. You will have to stay right with me so you don't get lost."

The boys looked at each other sideways. Lindell alternated between excitement (floor-to-ceiling food!) and apprehension (floor-to-ceiling food).

I saw their confused, almost frightened, faces in the rearview mirror.

"We will all be okay if we stick together," I said.

Inside, the first thing we had to do was apply for a membership. Ford looked cross, and in the absence of his father away on a military deployment, my oldest son took on the frugal-dad role.

"I do not agree with applying for entrance to this warehouse," Ford said. And when I took out my checkbook, he balked even more. "You're going to pay these people for the right to spend more money in their store?"

Next, I stood in front of the camera. All new members have to get their picture taken, and mine, of course, was as unattractive as any driver's license mug shot, but with the added "benefit" of three boys doing rabbit ears behind me.

Finally we entered the Disney World of food and other products. All four of us walked in silence. Could anyone really need that many writing pens? Were 50 rolls of toilet paper absolutely necessary? How long would it take to use 100 AA batteries anyway?

The tension broke when I discovered that our Sam's Club sells Smiley brand milk. Well, I just had to buy 4 gallons of that.

And juice boxes! How could I not buy 40?

High-fiber granola bars sold in packs of 30? Yes, please!

The biggest box of Cheerios I've ever seen? How could I not?

Soon our cart was overflowing and Ford was breaking into a sweat.

"Mom, where will we put all this?" he said. "What if we get tired of macaroni and cheese?"

I ignored him the same way I ignore Dustin.

"Mom, I have a bad feeling about this," Owen said.

Lindell begged for the bulk pack of king-size Hershey's bars.

It wasn't until I was loading the car that I began to have second thoughts. Sam's Club doesn't bag your groceries. Instead, you have the option to put your purchases in giant boxes. Now, I can make an Olympic sport of carrying the most plastic bags on my pinky finger, but I knew that even I would have to make multiple trips between the car and house when we got home from Sam's.

"And you paid to be able to do this," Ford said.

Lindell was mostly confused and happy until we got home. That's when he heard me say, "Where will I put all this macaroni and cheese?" and "Maybe I bought too much hand soap."

Lindell started to cry. "Mommy, I don't like that place. What if all this food takes up our whole house?"

"Yeah, I never want to go there again," Owen said.

"I can't believe you paid for this," Ford added.

Meanwhile, I shoved giant boxes into, above and below the pantry shelves. My heart beat faster. Sweat formed on my brow. As I wiped it away, I consoled myself. After all, it had seemed like such a good idea at the time.

THINGS I'LL FORGET

LAST WEEK, LINDELL FINISHED PRESCHOOL, WHICH MEANS next year he will begin kindergarten. I'm feeling sentimental about this, because I know, from watching Ford and Owen, that sons go into kindergarten as babies, and they come out as little boys. It is one of the most transformative years of school physically, mentally and emotionally.

I also have learned that mothering involves a near constant state of grieving. As children grow and change, they leave behind their former selves, and everything from their old voice to their baby-fine hair is gone forever.

Lindell—my wild and crazy little Lindell—is on the cusp of growing up.

So I'd like to document a few things. Another peculiar aspect of motherhood is that we tend to forget all the frustrating, difficult and obnoxious moments in exchange for everything we miss about our babies. In the fall, when I'm sad about Lindell beginning his journey through elementary school, I will need reminders of how thankful I should be.

For instance, I will forget how many times I had to watch the cartoon *Peppa Pig* after lunch when Lindell wasn't in school. Sure, *Peppa Pig* is hilarious. The pigs look like something my dog could draw, and when they laugh, they fall on the ground and roll on their big bellies. The youngest, baby-brother pig shoots tears horizontally out of his eyes when he cries. So there are worse things to have to watch. But usually, Lindell wants to watch the DVR, taped version—in reverse. He loves the way the baby brother's tears shoot back into his eyes and how the big daddy pig floats back onto his feet after a good laugh. Over and over again we watched that cartoon in reverse. And then we watched it some more. And I struggled to stay awake.

I also will forget how hard it was to get anything done with Lindell home half the day. Just as soon as I would start writing a column, he would yell from his bedroom, "I had an accident, Mommy, and I need new pants!" Or I'd try to clean the bathroom (mothers of boys know this is futile) and Lindell would spill his drink in the kitchen.

I'd take Lindell out to do errands, and everything took three times longer than necessary. I couldn't leave the grocery store without an epic battle over candy at the check-out aisle. At Target, he would whine for a new toy.

In the middle of a store without a public restroom, he'd suddenly need to use the bathroom.

I'd buckle his seat belt and it wouldn't "feel right."

I'd tie his shoes and his socks would be "all bumpy" on his toes.

Often I thought, "Man, I could get my whole to-do list done in an hour if I was alone."

And forget about doing anything for myself. Shopping for clothes meant that Lindell would crawl in and out of the dressing room, dragging bits of clothes with him, or he'd say, loud enough for anyone to hear, "What's that thing you always wear under your shirt, Mommy?"

At home, when he helped me make bread for dinner, he'd get the dough on his fingers and then the cupboard and all over the living room couch.

These are all the things I will forget as I watch my baby transform into a little boy. You'll show me this column, and I'll be disgusted at my former self, the one who wrote it. I'll think, "Gee, why did I write about all that stuff?"

Then I'll tell you all that I remember:

The way Lindell's chubby legs hung out of the shopping cart at Target, and how his perch there brought him eye-to-eye with me.

The way he ran down the aisles at the grocery store and the wind blew back his wispy hair.

How I'd look at him in the rearview mirror and see him mouthing the words to a song on the radio.

The time he looked at me in the mirror of a dressing room and said I was the most beautiful mommy ever.

The way he would run in and out of the clothes racks and hide behind a curtain of women's dresses. He always thought he was stealth, but I'd hear his giggle and spot his round cheeks peeking out from the clothes.

I'll tell you that our quiet lunches together at the kitchen table were thought-provoking and nearly meditative.

Our walks to get the older brothers at the end of the school day were always without incident and temper tantrums. Lindell stayed close by, his chubby hand in mine.

He never spilled milk or peed his pants. He kneaded the bread dough perfectly and always remembered to wash his hands after.

Then I'll tell you that I can still remember the way his head felt in the crook of my arm while we lay on the couch together watching *Peppa Pig*.

I'll recall the way his rounded belly rose and fell as he become more relaxed, and the way our breathing, together, became deeper and slower as we fell asleep snuggled together, the sound of baby-brother pig crying in the background.

I'll remember just these things. And I'll promise you that's exactly the way it was.

LINDELL LEARNING TO READ

LAST MONTH, MY YOUNGEST SON, LINDELL, BEGAN TO read. It was simple words at first. He noticed the "Open" sign in a window at the barber shop and the word "Sale" at the grocery store. Soon, however, he was asking for help with bigger words—"restaurant," "appointment," "excludes," "BOGO" ("BOGO?")—that he saw around him.

Before I could grasp what was happening, he called me into his bedroom and said, "I'll read the bedtime story to you tonight."

This means that I have no more babies, and my feelings are mixed.

On the one hand, it is fun to watch Lindell figure out the written world around him. His older brothers and I love to listen to him sound out words, like when he saw the word "office" and pronounced it "off-ice" at first.

"Try again," Ford, 12, said.

"Of-ice?" Lindell said. "Off-ise? No. Wait! Office! It's office!"

And on a recent trip to The Briar Patch, our favorite local bookstore, instead of rolling on the floor and making noise (his usual method of operation), Lindell ran to "his section" to find a book. He was so excited that the Mercy Watson series—the same one the school librarian reads to his class—is on "his level."

"You mean I can read Mercy Watson by myself?" he asked, his eyes wide and sparkling.

But written words are in many ways the final gatekeeper of innocence. They are the vehicle for grown-up conversation: "Will you please put them to B-E-D E-A-R-L-Y so that we can eat more D-E-S-S-E-R-T?" They are what allow parents to change the rules of Candy Land without any protests: "The rules say that if I draw a purple card twice, the game is over and it's time for bed." They are what keep young children like Lindell from accidentally reading the front page of the newspaper and learning what happened at Sandy Hook Elementary.

In the *Disappearance of Childhood*, Neil Postman argues that, in fact, the invention of the printed word is what created the concept of "childhood" to begin with. Words came to hold adult secrets that couldn't be unlocked until reading was mastered. Until then, children live in a blissful state, unburdened by things meant (i.e., written) only for adults.

I saw this with my oldest son, Ford, 12, who also started reading in kindergarten. Looking back, that's when he officially stopped being my little guy—the one who called me into his room for "one last story" and held my hand as we walked through a store, pointing with his other hand at things we passed ("What's that, Mommy?"). It was the tipping point to him heading down the path to independence. Today, he shuts himself in his room to read. He no longer asks for help with big words. He has his own email account.

Lindell is just beginning this process, and I am happy and sentimental.

There have been some truly funny moments, like when Lindell reads magazine headlines in the grocery store check-out line. Unlike older, wiser, well-read Ford, Lindell doesn't yet know that reading these out loud might be funny and inappropriate: "Look, Mom, that says, 'Saving myself for marriage,' and that says, 'pregnant by another man.'"

When we pass by the greeting card section, a real danger zone for mothers with emerging readers, Lindell reads everything that he can: "I wanted to get you a woman for your birthday. . . . Pull my finger. . . . This hot girl in a bikini has one wish for you . . ."

Many times, I have to intercept and tell him that he can't open the cards and read the inside. Unfortunately (fortunately?), this make him even more eager to learn new words.

But last week, when I overheard Owen coaching Lindell on the correct pronunciation of the word "other," things suddenly became very real. And kind of sad.

Lindell was reading aloud and said, "udder." Owen said, "It's time for you to start saying 'other,' not 'udder.'"

"Udder?" Lindell said.

"No, other."

"Udder."

"Say it with me, oth-her."

"Ud-der."

"No, other. Oth-her."

"Udder."

"Geez, Lindell, you sound like a baby."

I went into the room where both boys were reading in their beds. Owen nearly fills his up, and his bookshelf is stocked with thick, tattered books like Harry Potter and H.I.V.E.

Lindell looks like a little peanut in his big, twin bed. His bookshelf is filled with Mercy Watson and Dr. Seuss books that haven't had enough time to be tattered.

I kissed each boy on the top of his head as I turned out the reading lights. But when I got to Owen, I whispered in his ear, "Let's let him say 'udder' just a little bit longer. There is plenty of time for 'other.'"

DIARY OF A SNOW DAY

2:00 P.M. PRE-STORM: THE SCHOOL DEPARTMENT CANCELS school 18 hours before the first bell would ring. This almost never happens. The kids haven't even had a chance to go to bed with their pajamas on inside out. It's like someone has spilled the beans about a surprise birthday party.

There are two consequences. First, I can't force the kids to bed at 8 p.m., "just in case there is school tomorrow." The kids have been given a free Saturday night in the middle of the week. On the other hand, there won't be a cacophony of alarms and school-department messages tomorrow morning.

During all other snow storms, I knew, in the way that moms (especially moms with weather apps) know, that the kids probably wouldn't have school the next day. Yet I still made the kids—who didn't "just know"—go to bed at 8, "because you never know" (unless you have an hour-by-hour weather forecast). Then I stayed up late, watched "The Bachelor" and painted my toenails until midnight.

It was like a free weekend . . . until the next morning when the alert echoed from the answering machine, my cell phone rang and all of our text apps chimed.

6:00 p.m. pre-storm: Despite having been to the grocery store 24 hours earlier, I go again. If there is going to be a shortage of electricity and food, I won't be caught without my favorite pineapple fruit bars.

People are going crazy in the aisles. Water and bread are disappearing from the shelves. I roll my eyes, but by aisle seven, I'm throwing canned soup and non-perishable snacks into my basket. I contemplate freeze-dried food. I Google "how long will canned vegetables last in an apocalypse."

7:00 p.m. pre-storm: I tell the kids I'm too tired from the grocery store to make dinner. Side note: I never want to make dinner after I've been to the grocery store.

We order pizza.

10:00 p.m. pre-storm: The mainstream media is already beginning to downplay the Storm to End All Storms. My kids are wrestling each other upstairs. Lindell is literally sliding across the floor inside a laundry basket.

11:30 p.m. pre-storm: I fall asleep on the couch. I have my pajamas on the right way, hoping for a school day tomorrow.

8:00 a.m.: Six-foot snow drifts are no joke. You can lose a dog in drifts like that. Except, not our big, crazy hunting dog, who literally plows his way through the drifts, then runs back inside and shakes it all off onto the kitchen floor.

9:00 a.m.: The first "I'm bored" is heard in the Smiley house.

9:01 a.m.: I send the boys outside with shovels.

11:00 a.m.: The boys want to go sledding—in a blizzard. I wonder what part of "stay in your pajamas and watch movies all day" they don't understand.

Noon: I learn that the "horrible" snow day—you know, the one where they slept in, went sledding and ate leftover pizza—is my fault. Not coincidentally, everything else in the world is my fault, too. I'm a rotten mother.

12:30 p.m.: Everyone wants to eat. Again.

12:35 p.m.: I provide ice cream. I am the world's greatest mother.

2:00 p.m.: I'm guilted into playing Super Mario Bros. on the Wii because I "never, ever do anything fun with [my kids]. Not ever." I wonder why they've forgotten about the Pictionary game we played, and the ice cream! I am literally hoping for a power outage.

3:00 p.m.: I tell the kids I need to get work done. "But it's a snow day," they say.

4:00 p.m.: If I hear "we're bored" or "I'm hungry" one more time, I will scream something dramatic.

4:01 p.m.: Them: "We're bored."

Me: "Why do you guys even hope for snow days? You act miserable! Maybe you actually like school. Have you ever thought of that? Maybe you should hope for school days. I'm going to start sleeping with my pajamas on right every single night so that we never have a snow day again."

4:02 p.m.: I'm a terrible mother.

8:00 p.m.: I send everyone to their beds because, "there will be school tomorrow." If I have to go out and shovel the roads myself, there will be school tomorrow.

5:00 a.m. the next day: Cell phones are ringing. The answering machine is blaring. Texts are dinging. It's a snow day. Again.

I go downstairs, prepared to tell the kids that I will rip the Wii out of the wall and serve canned peas for lunch if they fight or whine once during the day.

But no one is there. They are all outside shoveling.

I go back to bed, satisfied that at least once, somewhere along the way, I must have done something right.

LINDIDDY

THE MOST PRESSING ISSUE AT OUR HOME RIGHT NOW IS this: Lindell's stuffed bird, Lindiddy, needs a bath, and no one can bring themselves to do it. Because no one wants Lindiddy to fall apart.

All of my children have had favorite stuffed animals during their childhoods, but none of those other "pets" have taken on the life that Lindiddy has. Lindiddy is effectively the seventh member of our family (with our dog Sparky being the sixth, of course). We don't speak ill of Lindiddy. Sometimes, he joins us at the dinner table. And if there was a fire, someone would probably grab him on the way out the door.

Lindiddy is not your typical stuffed animal. He's not a classic teddy bear or dog. He doesn't have a sweet face and sparkling eyes. No, Lindiddy is a lime-green jertin.

When he first came to us four years ago, Lindiddy had fluffy fur and a mohawk of green on top of his head. Through the years, his fur has become mashed, the mohawk matted. His eyes are sewn in, but the eyelids are drooping. His yellow nose is crooked, like he flew into a window. He has long, orange legs that are bent at the knees and flopping wing-like arms that are too long for his body.

When Lindell was still a baby, he carried Lindiddy by his long neck, pushing the stuffing up and down and leaving a hand-sized dent in the middle. Today, Lindiddy's head won't stand up straight due to this long ago injury.

Lindiddy came from the check-out counter at Kohl's. Dustin brought him home because *There's a Wocket in My Pocket* was, at that time, Lindell's favorite book. If I remember correctly, the purchase was partially a donation to a children's charity. This means that Lindiddy and his kin are not regular stock at Kohl's, nor anywhere else. Parents with children with favorite blankets or stuffed animals know this means no replacements.

These are the facts as I know them. According to Lindell, however, Lindiddy came from his parents' nest, which fell during a tornado. That's how Lindiddy broke his neck. He flew to safety at Kohl's, which is where Dustin found him. There is some speculation that Lindiddy once flew in World War II, but Lindell says that was just Lindiddy telling fibs. He has spoken to Lindiddy about this and says he won't lie again.

Sometimes, I wake up in the morning to Lindiddy "talking" to me: "Lindell's Mommy, you need to get up. It's 7 a.m." At hotels (yes, Lindiddy travels with us—in his own suitcase), Lindiddy hides in the curtains so that Lindell can say, "Look, he's a jertin in the curtain." Before we leave, someone always asks, "Does anybody have Lindiddy?"

Ford, 13, and Owen, 11, both had stuffed dogs. Ford's was named "Rocket," and Owen's "Just Puppy." I remember putting baby Ford and baby Owen to bed and resting their puppies in their arms before pulling up the blankets and tucking them under their chin. It was like a Christmas card. Putting Lindell to bed has an entirely different, Dr. Suesslike feel: he snuggles up against a lime-green bird with a mohawk on his head.

In preschool, Ford's "Rocket" fell in the toilet. We bought a replacement.

Owen's "Just Puppy" stayed in the hospital during Owen's tonsillectomy and had an emergency hot bath afterward to get rid of the germs. "Just Puppy" didn't survive the bath, so we got a replacement.

One of my greatest fears is that Lindiddy, with his bent neck and matted mohawk, would one day meet a similar fate and there would be no replacement. It's Lindell's fear, too.

So Lindiddy doesn't get bathed, though he desperately needs it. His fur smells soured from years of drool and sticky fingers mixed with the dirt and grime of travel. He's been accidentally stepped on in the car and left on the bathroom floor.

Recently, I decided it was time to save Lindiddy from becoming a biohazard. I convinced Lindell to let me give Lindiddy a bath. It would be a "bubble bath," we told him, and very gentle. Lindell's older brothers rolled their eyes as if to say, "He's just an old stuffed animal!"

"I know, I know," I whispered to them as I walked by.

But then, in the basement, as I got ready to throw the stuffed bird into the washing machine, I stopped. I pictured Lindiddy's drooping eyelids staring out at me as they go round and round in the soapy water. I pictured Lindiddy banging on the glass with his oversized wing-arms to get out. Then I pictured him staring at me again from the dryer: "Save me! It's hot in here!"

I came back upstairs with Lindiddy cradled in my arms.

"Mom!" Ford and Owen yelled.

"Hey, if you saw the way Lindiddy looked at me," I told them, "you couldn't do it either."

A Letter to My Future Daughters-in-Law

Dear future daughters-in-law,

I have you in mind quite a bit. I am keenly aware that my three boys will live with me for a mere 18 years and with you for a lifetime. My successes and missteps impact your future. I know this because I live with a man who says his mom told him he could do anything—even sing [shudder].

One time, Dustin and I made lists of the parts of our egos and self-confidence that are sensitive to criticism. The goal was to learn where each of us is likely to be defensive. I had three items on mine: being a mother, writing and my weight. Dustin can make fun of my cooking and cleaning all he wants. I take no pride in those things, and I don't claim to be good at them. But Dustin should choose his words wisely when treading on the Big Three.

Dustin's list was a tad longer, and by "a tad" I mean that when he handed me his list of All Things Important to My Confidence, it fell open to the floor like a grandmother's accordion-style wallet filled with the grandkids' photos.

"You can't feel like you do all of these things well," I said, scanning the list. "Singing? You put singing on here?"

"My mom said I'm the best at all of those," he said.

And ever since, it has been my job to cross off Dustin's "talents" (he simply couldn't claim "cooking"), and make the list a bit more manageable.

Dustin's mom, however, raised him to be incredibly giving, patient, smart, loving and understanding. So there's that. But she was wrong about the singing.

As a father, Dustin has been a great example, and I have no doubt my boys will also be giving, patient, smart, loving, understanding—and totally handsome. Still, I'm working to correct other things that are likely to plague you. Like toilet seats. How many times do we have to go over it: toilet seat up. Toilet seat down. Wash hands. Replace the hand towel on bar, not the floor. Turn off the light.

The boys also leave their dirty clothes completely intact in the laundry basket. Do you know how gross it is to unravel a sweaty baseball sock? It's as if the boys slither out of their clothes, like a snake shedding its skin, and place the now flattened pants, underwear and socks, all still connected, into the basket. No, they don't take the gum or change out of their pockets, either. We're working on that. (Question: What's worse than sending a pack of bubblegum through the dryer? Answer: Nothing.) The boys also burp and make strange jokes. Gosh, I hope you think those are funny.

And then there are each boy's individual quirks. Take Ford, for instance. If there's one thing you should know about Ford, it is this: When playing a game that Ford created (and he creates a lot of them), you will always lose. Don't bother trying. Ford made the rules, and you will lose. If Ford makes an IQ test for you, you will fail that, too. Not because you aren't smart. I'm sure that you are. No, you will fail because Ford is grading it. Ford likes being right. And just like his dad, he usually ends up being so. It's frustrating, I know.

Owen is the middle child—that should tell you enough. Maybe it's why you love him. He once fell asleep in the garage while playing hide-and-go-seek, and he moves through the house like a cat. Startling. But Owen is the ultimate consumer. His favorite part of everything is buying something new. New baseball season? New glove. New school year? New backpack. Don't give him access to your Amazon account.

And then there's Lindell. Oh, Lindell's wife, what can I say? By the time you read this, I will have already shown you the video of Lindell dancing like a T-Rex or running around the baseball field in a barely big enough lion costume. I do hope he has given up the lion outfit by the time he's yours. Lindell wants your name to be Buckachewy. He plans to use that nickname if it isn't. And I hope you don't mind living with an invisible robot named Bob. Bob has been Lindell's imaginary friend since he was 3. You will need to set a place at the table for him. Sorry.

Don't worry, I still have some years left with these guys. We are working out the kinks. My goal is to raise three boys so that you will live a happy life with a man—a man who will be strong and kind but will never stop making you laugh, like my Dustin. (Ask him to sing "If You Leave Me Now" by Chicago.)

And, please, remember this: I am so glad to have more females in the family.

The Fairness of World—and Coin Tosses

IF YOU HAVE MULTIPLE CHILDREN, YOU KNOW THE WORST situation a parent can have: there are several options, but only one that is good, and everyone wants it. It doesn't even matter if that option really isn't good by adult standards. As soon as one child says he desperately wants it, that he will go in his room if he doesn't get it, every other child thinks that option is as fantastic as a winning lottery ticket.

My older brother Will (he has one child) experienced this firsthand during his family's recent trip to Maine. Will and I were taking the kids canoeing, and although we have just one canoe, we have three paddles. Two of them are metal and considered by most adults to be the "better paddles." Indeed, Dustin and I paid good money for them.

The third paddle is wooden and was found under an old shed. It very likely was someone else's trash. Still, everyone under the age of 30 that day wanted the splintered, wooden paddle. What's more, they all wanted to sit in the back of the canoe, too.

I watched amused as my brother maneuvered this dangerous territory. By the end of it, I could see in his eyes that he was tempted to go out into my dad's work shed and build another wooden paddle.

Will looked to me for help because the canoe trip was actually my idea. In about 45 minutes the sun would set on the western side of the lake, and I was positive it would be as spectacular as the night before, when the sun bounced maroon and golden hues off the clouds and across the water. Only Dustin and I went on that sunset paddle. It was quiet, beautiful and romantic. Surely this sunset would be the same if I went with four children, right?

"How about one of you take the wooden paddle on the trip out," Will said, "and then you switch?"

Sounds reasonable. Unless you're younger than 16.

"And what about the seats?" Owen said. "Who gets to sit in the back?"

"One of you will sit in the back on the way there, and one of you will sit in the back when we come home," Will said.

My children stared at him. Did he really think it could be solved that easily?

"I'm older, so I get the wooden paddle and the back seat both ways," Ford said.

"No way," Owen yelled.

(Meanwhile, the sun was beginning to slip further toward the horizon.)

"I know," Will said triumphantly, "Let's flip a coin."

That sounded easy, too. Then Will realized we needed to flip four times: twice for the seat (there and back) and twice for the paddle (there and back), because Ford thought it was not reasonable to flip once and then give the return trip/paddle to the loser. That's because Ford was sure he would win by choosing heads, which has, according to him, a "50.37% chance of winning every flip."

Owen claimed tails, and apparently, the world was on our side. The flips for the paddle ended fairly: Ford would have it one way and Owen the other.

Will threw the coin up again. It seemed to flip in slow motion. Everyone came closer. Will uncovered the coin. Ford won the back seat for the trip out. So far, fate agreed with the fairest of options: split everything.

"Do you really want me to flip a fourth time?" Will said looking at me. His eyes were pleading.

"You have to," Ford said. "It's the only way."

Flipping again, of course, meant that Owen (tails) might lose his chance to sit in the back of the canoe both ways.

Will flipped the coin. It seemed to beat the air as it spun. Inside, I yelled, "NOOOOOOOOOO," in one long, drawn-out breath. I have never wanted to see tails on a coin so badly before.

Will caught the coin on the back of his hand, took a deep breath and uncovered it.

Heads.

What happened next is a story that should be stored away, never to see the light of day until my kids are getting married and I need to embarrass them.

Amazingly, the sun was not waiting for this nonsense.

By this point, no one even remembered what they were fighting for. But Will, as the uncle, knew he had to fix it. I might never know what magic he worked that night, but ten minutes later, everyone was happily getting in the canoe.

We raced to a small island, where we hoped to watch the sun's show. But the universe, of course, had the last word in this drama: The sun unceremoniously, and without even a hint of maroon, slipped below the horizon and left me and my brother sitting there with kids bickering about who was wearing the other's shorts.

Letting Go of the Bike

The second-biggest secret parents keep from their children is this: Training wheels in no way truly prepare you for riding a bike alone. They just don't.

This is what makes learning to ride a bike so unforgettable. The entire process is unnatural. There is no way to ease into it, because it takes speed and faith to keep a bike balanced. Sure, there are the aforementioned training wheels and metal bars for a parent to hold, but a child cannot balance on his own two wheels until he is actually doing it.

It's like walking: Either you're walking, or you're just standing there. There isn't much in-between room. This is why we always remember a child's first steps. The instant he lets go of the couch and trusts that his right leg will follow the left is a miraculous thing. No one can make a child do it. It just happens.

I was truly horrified when Ford learned to ride a bike eight years ago. I actually needed to go inside and let Dustin handle the lessons. In one afternoon, my firstborn child became intimately familiar with the pavement—except for the time he catapulted himself forward off the bike and landed in a bush.

Things were different when Owen learned to ride a bike. While Ford goes at life full throttle, Owen is a bit more cautious. He would like you to jump off the rock into the lake before he tries it. And even then, peer pressure is no match for Owen's will of steel. He seemed to look at the two-wheeled contraption we bought for him and say, "If God had wanted us to ride bikes, wouldn't he have built them?"

Again, I asked Dustin to handle the lessons. I couldn't watch.

Turns out, however, there was nothing to watch. Owen wasn't having any part of this "balance on two spinning wheels" thing.

He did like the helmet, though.

Then one day, Ford came running into the house. "Come outside and see Owen," he said.

I stepped onto the front porch, and, just like that, Owen was riding his bike without training wheels. Ford had taught him.

I hoped the same thing would happen with Lindell. If Owen has a will of steel, Lindell's is super-glued, secured with plastic ties and locked down with a deadbolt that I assure you has no key. Seriously, we've tried all the tricks: bribes, pressure, chocolate. When Lindell doesn't want do something, not even a cupcake will convince him. When you try to put him on a boat, he is like the dog that literally shimmies its head out of the collar. He can make his legs turn to jelly like nobody's business, or he can make his body as stiff as a board—really unwelcome when he was younger and we tried to get him in his carseat. If all else fails, there's always screaming. And Lindell can scream.

In other words, I would eat rotten asparagus before I'd try to teach my youngest how to ride a bike.

But Dustin gave it a shot.

They did the training wheels and the metal bar sticking off the back. Lindell played along for a couple of years, probably just to see his dad running up and down the street. Riding bikes was always a "dad thing" for Lindell. "I'll try again when dad is home," he'd say. It was like Lindell could smell my fear.

Then one day he said, "Mom, it's time for you to teach me how to ride my bike." I started to explain that no one can really learn how to ride a bike. You just need to do it. But saying that goes against every sort of parent code. It's best to let them think the training wheels will somehow make it all easier.

So we went outside, and I reluctantly ran up and down our street holding on to the back of Lindell's bicycle seat. There is a video of this, and it's not attractive. No one runs gracefully when they have one hand fixed to a seat. We went back and forth, up and down, until sweat ran down my temples.

And then I let go. But Lindell didn't know it. He rode to the end of the street by himself. When he stopped and turned around, I yelled, "See? You did it!"

Lindell was angry I had let go.

All I felt was sad. My last child can ride a bike. There is no one to run behind, no bicycle seat to hold. Yes, I had released the bike, but I knew it was Lindell who was letting go. He did it so naturally, and yet it felt so unnatural to me.

Which, of course, is the first biggest secret parents keep from their children: We never really wanted to let go.

A Sad, Backward Version of
The Very Hungry Caterpillar

I'll begin at the end: By the time the boys returned to school after the holiday break, Dustin told them, "If your teachers ask you to draw what you did over vacation, draw a silver bowl and tell them, 'Take from this what you will.'"

Put a broken iPhone in the silver bowl, and that pretty much sums up our New Year's.

Two weeks before, we had one of our best Christmases ever. After three years of being "just the five of us," we finally had family in town to celebrate with us. Plus, Santa actually remembered to bring Ford a globe—it only took seven years of asking—and gave him an iPhone, too.

The phone was especially exciting, because Dustin and I said we'd never buy him one. That was before the salesman at AT&T, working magic I still don't understand, lowered our monthly bill with the addition of another line. Otherwise, Santa would be in a heap of trouble for getting us into a contract.

Two days after Christmas, we followed Dustin to Washington, D.C., where he'd be working over New Year's and where we keep a small—like, really small—apartment. We planned a trip to Monticello and maybe a few days with my parents. But on the first day, we rested. We watched movies all day and played with new Christmas toys.

I remember saying to Dustin, "It's nice to have a down day like this, but I can't stay cooped up in the apartment all week."

About two hours later, I got sick—all over the only bathroom in the place.

For the next two days, I was bedridden. The kids were living like *Home Alone* outside the one-bedroom apartment while Dustin worked all day. Pizza boxes piled up in the kitchen, and when Dustin came home at night he had to do about four loads of laundry in the coin-operated machines down the hall.

On Tuesday, once I was better, we were really ready for that trip to Monticello.

That's when Owen got sick—all over the only bathroom in the place.

Two days and four loads of laundry later, Owen was feeling better.

That's when Lindell got sick. All over the only bath— well, actually, he never made it to the bathroom.

Two days and four loads of laundry after that, it was time to drive back to Maine.

That's when Ford got sick.

It was like a really sad version of *The Very Hungry Caterpillar.*

On our way home, I had planned to stay at a hotel in Massachusetts that offers a big brunch and an indoor pool. It would be the consolation prize for having driven 12 hours to spend a week in the one-bedroom apartment. But when Ford got sick, I knew I had to cancel and possibly face financial penalties.

Luckily, the woman on the phone let us cancel with a 100 percent refund.

"I can't thank you enough," I told her. "Your kindness is a bright spot in a bad week."

Looking back on it, what I should have said to her is this: "I can't thank you enough because I'm about to put a $550 phone in the washing machine, so I'm going to need that money."

I hung up the phone, stripped the bed and headed to the coin-operated laundry machine for what I hoped would be the last time.

"All this laundry is getting really expensive," Dustin said.

At that very moment, we were shoving Ford's brand new iPhone, lost in a tangled blanket, into the washer.

When I got back to the apartment, Ford said he couldn't find his phone.

"Oh, I have this handy app called 'Find my iPhone,'" I told him cheerfully. I few quick taps later, and the app was loading. "We'll just click to update, and—"

Ford watched over my shoulder as the screen refreshed. My iPhone appeared first, in the apartment, where it should be. Dustin's appeared next, right next to mine. And then Ford's phone lit up—down the hall.

"Does that seem like it's near the washing—?"

"Nooooooooooooooooo!"

I ran to the washing machine, but it was too late. The door was locked. On the app, Ford's phone still glowed, until the last 10 minutes of the cycle, when it went black.

"I hope Santa got insurance," Dustin said.

I looked at him and cried. I mean, who gets the insurance? (Moral of this story: Get the insurance.)

Ford handled the whole thing surprisingly well. Mostly, he was relieved the accident wasn't his fault. Also, there was the hope that Chris from Chris Downs Computer Room could help.

Lindell, however, didn't understand what all the fuss was about. "Why is everyone so upset," he said. "I mean, just be glad Santa bought the phone, not you."

Yes, well, there's always that.

I Ruined Halloween

I ruined my oldest son's experiences with Hallow-een. I regret that. But maybe by sharing my story, I can help you not to ruin your child's experience.

Parenting is scary stuff, and our society is full of fear. I drank that Kool-Aid once. I believed my son might be kid-napped while trick-or-treating or that a neighbor might slip a needle into his chocolate candy bar. (Has that ever really happened?) If Ford snuck a piece of candy from his bag before I inspected it, I'd nearly have a heart attack on the sidewalk. Now he's going to die!

You see, I thought that Halloween was about little kids. And by that I mean, I thought it was about what the parents of little kids want Halloween to be about. Turns out, how-ever, Halloween is really for the older kids. (I know. Bear with me.)

It all began in Florida. That's where Ford spent most of his first Halloweens. While he had no voice (literally) or opinion, I dressed him in Winnie the Pooh and Thomas the Tank costumes. Because Ford was my first child, I got away with this for many years, until my second child, Owen, arrived and was forced to wear the Winnie the Pooh and Thomas the Tank costumes.

Ford has no good memories of these Halloweens. It didn't help that I made the boys' costumes myself using double-thick felt that isn't known for being super breathable.

In Florida's 100-degree October temperatures, this was a problem. Also, the Flash costume I made Owen was so small, the inseam pushed his diaper completely to one side. He looked like he had messed one side of his pants.

We'd walk to a few houses, with the boys always in my sight. Sometimes I even walked up to the neighbors' doors with them. I held the pail of candy, guarding it with my life so that neither of my boys could possibly eat a tainted, needle-laced piece. I put reflector tape on their shoes and Winnie-the-Pooh ears, and I put an emergency whistle around their necks. I stopped just short of driving the boys to each individual house.

Eventually, Ford and Owen wanted to wear costumes they picked out. Also, they wanted to wear ones that I didn't make. In fact, they didn't want me to have any part of the costume decision making. This began the era of *Star Wars*. From the time I released my costume control to Ford until about three years ago, he and Owen only dressed as *Star Wars* characters for Halloween.

The *Star Wars* era also coincided with the boys not wanting me to walk up to the neighbors' doors with them. The boys suggested I wait by the curb—someone else's curb. But I followed behind, like a creeper in the bushes, always vigilant against poisoned candy. I wanted to take them to "safer" Halloweens inside stores or nearby gyms. But apparently I was missing the point of Oct. 31.

Last year, when Ford was nearly 13, I gave up completely. Ford and Owen ran off with their friends, and I didn't see them again until 9 p.m. According to Ford, it was his best Halloween ever. Of course, it's important to note that my boys are good kids. They aren't stealing people's candy or egging houses. No, they are putting on funny mustaches, using British accents, and running through the neighborhood (ours happens to be very safe) at dark with their friends.

And maybe that is what Halloween is about: Pre-teens practicing independence in a controlled environment.

Actually, though, isn't that what Halloween always was about until helicopter parenting came en vogue? I don't remember my mom ever walking with me while I went trick-or-treating. I'm sure she did when I was really young, but I trick-or-treated until I was about 13, and I have no memories of my Mom being there. I only remember running around with my friend Leslie, eating too much sugar and feeling like a rebel because I was out at 8 p.m. on a school night.

I know, people sigh when they open the door and see lanky, awkward teenagers standing on the stoop asking for candy. We think, "aren't they too old for this?" and "Halloween is for the kids!" I felt the same way until I had a new teenager of my own. Now, however, when I open the door and see an absolutely clueless two-year-old waiting there, his mother close by with the bucket of candy, I think, "Where are the kids who are flexing their wings, running around with their friends?"

We mothers try to control everything else, but for one night, on the eve of November, the neighborhood opens up to young boys and girls who don't need to hold their mom's hand and are practicing to be adults (well, besides the fez and bag of candy). Perhaps Halloween really is the only holiday specifically for them.

LIVING WITH ALL BOYS

WHEN I MARRIED MY HUSBAND, DUSTIN, THERE WERE certain things I knew about him. I knew he leaves his keys wherever he feels like it and can't find them later. I knew that, left to his own devices, Dustin will put his spoons in one kitchen drawer and his forks in another. I even knew he has the unusual ability to fall asleep anywhere—even on a park bench at Disney World.

And I decided to marry him anyway.

Maybe I thought I could change these things. Maybe I loved Dustin for them—or in spite of them. In any case, what I didn't foresee way back then was that our three boys would end up just like Dustin. No, I didn't give that a lot of thought.

Of course, who knew we would have three boys? Answer: I did. After Ford was born, I said, "Gosh, we are on a roll of having all boys."

"One boy does not make a 'roll,'" Dustin said.

After Owen was born, I asked, "Are we on a roll now?"

"The chances are still 50/50 every time," he said.

Fifteen years and three sons later, I am completely outnumbered and, frankly, fighting a losing battle. Even the dog is male.

I live in a house with people who lose things and then yell, "Where's my [baseball, jacket, hat, homework]?" I used to rush to their aid, but I stopped when every time I arrived by their side, eager to help, I found them standing in the middle of a room, staring at nothing.

"I can't find it," they say.

"Where have you looked?" I ask.

That's when they look at me, like, "I'm supposed to look?"

I truly believe Dustin thinks merely standing in a room will cause lost objects to appear. And forget about asking any of them to find something for me.

ME: Can you go get my coat from the kitchen?

THEM (aka, everyone else I live with): OK, but where in the kitchen?

ME: I don't know. It's a coat. I don't think it's hiding.

THEM: Yeah, but where should I look?

ME: In the kitchen.

THEM: Where?

ME: Probably in the toaster.

THEM: OK, I'll try.

These people I live with also have a different understanding of cleanliness and personal hygiene. Mold on bread can be cut out. Week-old pizza is still good. A hole with socks in it can still provide a few more weeks of drafty foot covering. Did I teach them nothing?

ME: Did you wash your hands?

OWEN: Yes—yesterday.

Random, used flossers—you're welcome, Dr. Rand—lie on the end tables in our living room. Toenail clippings are in the bathroom sink. And, please, let's not even discuss the bathroom floor.

All of this, by the way, is why scented candles are so popular with women.

It's like I'm living with cavemen half the time. Dustin promises me the Smiley men are evolving. He does a great impression of the evolutionary chart and what he and his ancestors might look like on it. But maybe I'll see this evolution in hindsight.

Until then, I think I'm devolving.

Every day, I put my keys in the exact same spot. I always know where they are. Except for last Tuesday. My keys were missing. I ran from room to room, staring at nothing and yelling, "Where are my keys? I can't find them?"

THEM: Did you look in the bathroom?

ME: Yes, I stood in that room and stared at nothing for at least five minutes.

THEM: Did you look in the kitchen?

ME: Why would my keys be in the kitchen? That's where I keep my coat.

Then my youngest, Lindell, said, "Do you think they are in the car?"

That's when I turned around and snapped, "If I thought they were in the car, do you think I'd be here looking in the house?"

The keys actually were in the car, but that didn't matter. Before I found them, I'd stomp around the house some more and yelled, "Where are my keys? Why won't anyone help me find my keys?"

Ford lay on the small couch, flossing his teeth—you're welcome again, Dr. Rand. His dirty feet were propped up on the side table next to his other used flosser. Owen lay on the larger couch in yesterday's gym shorts, the ones that are unraveling from the hem.

"All you do is sit there," I yelled. "No one helps me with anything. And have you seen your bathroom lately? Believe me, I saw it when I was in there staring at nothing and looking for my keys. Get up and make your bed or something. Gosh!"

I stomped up the stairs and closed my bedroom door.

Ford yelled up at me, "Geez, why do women always have to be so cranky?"

MANAGING CHILDREN, GARDENS

LAST WEEK, DUSTIN AND I LEFT MAINE, A PLACE THAT often feels insulated, in a good way, from the negative aspects of big-city living, and traveled to Washington, D.C., and Hampton Roads, Va., to visit family. While there, I spoke at a military-spouse event, and a woman in the audience told me that her children, who are now grown but were raised in the military and had made dozens of moves during their childhood, each considered a different city to be their home.

This led Dustin and me to have a familiar debate about where to raise our children. It's a debate that is somewhat beside the point for military families who usually don't have control over where they will live and for how long. In any case, Dustin and I asked ourselves, is it better to expose our children to different experiences and environments, perhaps at the risk of diluting their sense of place, or to have roots in a "hometown"? Or is it better to give our children one city, one house, one community to come back to and say, "This—this very place—is where my brothers and I grew up"

"I think kids are a lot like seedlings," Dustin said as we drove along I-95, headed for Hampton Roads. "You can't just take seeds that are started indoors and put them in the ground. You have to expose them, little by little, to the elements first."

Just before we left for our vacation, I had done that very thing with a tray full of seedlings. The leggy sprouts with delicate leaves had never been exposed to wind, rain or extremes in temperature. For their entire existence thus far they sat on the windowsill in my boys' bedroom, insulated from the outdoors, yet still able to soak in the sunlight. As the new plants grew taller and their roots began to crowd the small container, the stems arched, at first almost imperceptibly, and then later with astonishing aggressiveness, toward the light coming through the glass. It was as if they were almost begging to get out of their cramped pots and spot upon the sill.

So I took the trays outside for a few hours at a time at first, and never at night. I watered them, made sure they were warm and then explicitly and methodically exposed them to the harsher environments that they eventually would need to stand up against. Once I was sure that the plants could handle it, I left the tray outside overnight. I let the rain pound the thin stalks down against the dirt. And then I carefully took each one out of its container, made a hole in the ground and set the plants free in the garden.

I suppose Dustin is right. I'd like to be able to do the same thing for my children. I'd like to shield them from the world while at the same time pruning their branches and keeping the soil free of weeds. However, as any gardener (or parent) knows, even the best weed prevention is no match for the yellow dandelions of spring, whose roots are as big as industrial rubber bands and seem to grow from and grab hold of the very bottom of the Earth. My tray of seedlings needed extra attention, bordering on coddling, in order to thrive. But an unwanted weed? Well, those seemingly pop up overnight despite your robbing them of sunlight and water. If a tiny dot of poison makes its way onto a seedling's tender leaves, it will kill it. Yet a gallon of poison often isn't enough for the largest dandelions.

I also had sprayed our yard for weeds before our vacation. When I came home a week later, I found that the weeds were mostly gone, and so was a large section of grass. It's the same way with the kids: I teach them one thing (don't talk to strangers), only to unwittingly stamp out another. ("Why didn't you answer that nice lady at church when she talked to you?" "Because you told me not to talk to strangers, Mom.")

Yes, both children and gardens are incredibly fickle things to manage, but as important and necessary to this world as the air we breathe. It seems deceptively easy to get it right when you and your husband are sitting in an air-conditioned car comparing and contrasting big-city living with small-town life. And yet gardens also can be like raising children when many seasons later, after noticing all the weeds you meant to pull but eventually overlooked, or the bare ground where you thought you'd plant some flowers but never did, you realize that your garden hasn't necessarily been growing because of your best intentions. Indeed, oftentimes it has been growing despite them.

It Will be Quiet All too Soon

People tell me that although raising three boys seems "tiring" (their word, not mine; I would have chosen something stronger) right now, the boys' childhood will pass quicker than I might expect.

It didn't seem that way last Saturday when Dustin and I took the boys to a high school baseball game. The stadium is just a few blocks from our house, so we walked. Well, Dustin and I walked. Ford rode his bike (the one he can't get started by himself), Owen rode his Big Wheel (the one that requires a push every few feet), and just to fit in, Lindell took his push-cart (the one he used when learning to walk). By the time we got to the field, Dustin and I were responsible for carrying all three forms of transportation, and we alternated duty with Lindell on our shoulders.

It seemed as if our three young boys were a tornado between us. In fact, I don't remember talking to Dustin at all during the game. We were too busy chasing kids. Afterward, we had plans to take the boys for ice cream, but once we dragged the bike, Big Wheel and push-cart home and broke up a few fights along the way, we were too tired to think about it. The boys, of course, went about their business wrestling in the backyard. They came inside only occasionally to say, "He hit me!" "He looked at me funny" or "He took my baseball bat."

The next day, we took the boys to church. It was a special service honoring local graduates, and three high school seniors gave the sermon. Two of the seniors were males. Stuck in the space between being a boy and a grown man, they had broad but skinny shoulders, smooth faces, long arms and legs, and voices that sometimes cracked. At once they seemed like someone's baby, and then I saw glimpses of the men they are becoming.

There was a time when I would have identified with the seniors onstage. But on that Sunday, I identified with the seniors' mothers, wherever they sat in the church. Could those mothers remember days like the one we had just had at the ballpark? Did it seem like only yesterday to them? Now that their boys were grown, had the mothers finally gotten all the stains out of their furniture and the smell of dirty socks and shoes out of the closets? Did they have Play-Doh in their cabinets? Was dried-up syrup smeared beneath the kitchen table? How long had it been since they changed a diaper? Put a Band-Aid on a knee?

When was the last time those long, lanky boys with Adam's apples curled into the side of their mother and laid their head on her shoulder?

The children in the congregation were excused for Sunday school. I walked Ford and Owen to their classroom, and on the way back into the sanctuary, climbed a set of stairs. Purely by reflex, I put out my right palm, as if to catch the hand of a toddler and help them up the steps. For almost a decade, a pudgy hand has reached up for mine at every flight of stairs or to cross the street. For almost a decade, there has been no me without them. But on this day, there was no one to help.

Not knowing what else to do with my hands, I tucked them into my pockets, removing them only to wipe away a small tear before I took my seat in the sanctuary again.

At the baseball game last Saturday, I sat for a moment behind my oldest boys as they knelt on the concrete and pressed their faces to the chain-link fence to get a better look at the game. They desperately wanted to catch a foul ball. For all their new long, awkward legs and knobby knees, Ford and Owen looked like babies in the shadows of the young men on the field. They watched with their mouths held open in perfect O's.

One of the players on deck noticed my boys watching him from above. He turned around and smiled, then gave them a quick thumbs up. Later he passed them a ball through the fence.

Yes, someday my boys will be all grown up. I'll be somewhere in the stands or the pews, alone with my peace and quiet, and feeling sad because I don't have a bike to push home. Maybe I won't even remember the last time I kissed a bruised knee. But if my boys grow up to be the kind of young men who turn around and smile at two little kids in the stands, it all will have been worth it. And when they have their own little "tornadoes," I will smile and laugh, because I get to send those back home to their mothers.

STAR WARS IS TEARING US APART

In the 10 years that we have been a family, there have been two instances that nearly ripped us apart: the time that Lindell, 3, erased his older brothers' Super Mario Bros. Wii profile and the day that no one wanted to give anyone the *Star Wars* Tatooine skiff because they wanted it for themselves.

The former happened last week. Ford, 9, and Owen, 7, completed all eight worlds of Mario and had unlocked world nine, a secret bonus level. The celebration surrounding this was comparable to that of a Super Bowl victory. Soon after, however, Lindell took an interest in the sleek, white Wii controllers. Through no small feat of his own, Lindell created his own profile on Mario, copied it to the boys', pressed save and erased everything.

I was at school when this happened, but according to Ford's play-by-play account, Lindell did it while his brothers watched. They just weren't quick enough to do the usual: tackle Lindell to the ground before he hit save. Ford described the look on Lindell's face afterward as "one of satisfaction," which, once Ford and Owen started screaming, morphed into the classic, guilty Lindell look: eyes shifted to one side to avoid contact, eyebrows raised, lips pursed and pushed to the opposite side of his gaze.

When I got home from school, the kids were already in bed, but Dustin re-enacted the apocalyptic drama for me.

He raised his arms and his face to the heavens, dropped to his knees and wailed, "Why? Why? WHY? How will we go on? How will we survive?" According to Dustin, he wasn't sure the boys could withstand the disaster. Which reminded me of the first time our family was almost torn apart.

Two Christmases ago, I bought online a toy *Star Wars* Tatooine skiff (a flying boat of sorts used to take prisoners to the sarlacc), one that isn't manufactured anymore. I had planned for Owen to give it to Ford as a gift. When I brought Owen into my room to help wrap it, however, it was the first time he had actually seen a toy skiff. He fell into a heap on the floor.

"But I want the skiff," he cried. "I've always wanted a skiff, and they don't make them anymore!"

At first I had sympathy for Owen. I remember being 7 years old and wanting a life-size stuffed husky so bad that I would have been willing to sell all my Barbies in a garage sale for it. I rubbed Owen's back as he cried into the floor and tried to help him understand the spirit of giving: "Won't it be fun, then, to give your brother such an excellent gift? Imagine how excited he will be!"

Owen wasn't buying it, and I eventually lost my patience. "If you're going to be spoiled and selfish, then just leave the room," I said. I put the skiff back in my closet and called Ford up to the room. Ford and Owen passed on the stairway. Owen's tear-stained face caused Ford to walk cautiously through the door.

"I bought something for Owen to give to you," I said. "But he wants it for himself."

Owen was still wailing downstairs.

"Since you are older and understand that you and Owen share everything anyway, I thought you might want to give the gift to Owen instead."

I opened the closet door, stuck my head in a curtain of hanging clothes, and pulled out the skiff.

"What?" Ford screamed. "A skiff? I've always wanted a skiff."

Now he was on the floor crying, too.

Dustin came to see what I had done to devastate both boys in a matter of minutes. I explained and pulled the skiff out from the closet again. Dustin fell to his knees and cried, "Nooooooo! I want it!" He was mocking the boys, but when he had finished the parody, he said, "No really, that's pretty cool. Let me see it." Still admiring the skiff, he said, "A long time from now, they will say, 'The Smileys were such a nice family—until the Tatooine skiff came into their lives.'"

He didn't know the half of it. While working on this column, I searched "Tatooine skiff" to check the spelling. Turns out the toy, in its unopened box, is quite collectible. One site claims you could buy a car with the value of it.

When I realized the skiff that everyone in our family once coveted now lies in pieces at the bottom of a toy chest and that the box is long gone, I channeled Luke Skywalker hanging from the reactor shaft generator in the middle of Cloud City and screamed at my computer, "No! Nooooo! That's not true. That's impossible!"

Yellow Beans

RECENTLY AT A CHURCH DINNER, I TOLD MY BOYS, "THERE will be a limit on the bread." What I meant was that each of them could have two pieces with their lasagna. This was a result of the week before, when my almost-11-year-old son brought his plate to the table with a half loaf of french bread on it. (Side note: College savings are nice, but lately I wonder if Dustin and I should have started a savings account to pay for groceries when we eventually have three teenage boys in the house.)

"A limit?" Ford said. "I'll starve!"

Suddenly Lindell started to cry. But his whimpers were mere background noise because I was busy telling Ford to put his knees down and bring his chair closer to the table.

Lindell pulled at my shoulder. That's when I turned around and saw his red, wet eyes. But I was still frustrated by his whining and pestering.

"My gosh, Lindell, what is it?" I said.

"Who will take it off for me?" he cried.

"What? Take what off for you?"

"The lemon. I don't want a lemon on my bread."

This past summer, Lindell took swimming lessons—again. He is still in Level 1, which is to say he sits on the side of the pool, arms folded across his chest, and refuses to get in the water. At the end of the two weeks, we are presented with a certificate for Lindell's "participation" and the recommendation that he take Level 1—again—next summer. We fear he will one day be the only boy in Level 1 who shaves.

But the instructors are very patient. They continue to try, with endless enthusiasm, to get Lindell into the water.

One day Lindell ran away from his teacher, back to the safety of the grass and his towel, crying, "I don't wanna put my face in the water! I don't wanna put my face in the water!"

The teacher took him by the hand, and while she gently guided him back toward the pool, she said, "Let's not worry about that now. Just get your feet in the pool. Don't think about putting your face in. We'll cross that bridge when we come to it."

Lindell stopped and thought about that. Then he said, "OK, but before I go, what bridge are you talking about?"

At least we know his answer to, "If your friend jumped off a bridge . . ."

About a year ago, Lindell listened patiently to an intense discussion between Dustin and Ford about space. For about 10 minutes they debated the possibility of other life forms in our galaxy and the feasibility of parallel universes outside of our own. When Ford mentioned the Milky Way, Lindell suddenly was interested.

"Wait a minute," he said slowly, his face full of intrigue. "You're telling me there are candy bars just floating around in space?"

This was science Lindell could get excited about!

Over the years we've learned to adapt to these Lindell-lisms. Indeed, I could draw a special map of our city with Big Donald's on one corner and a few streets away, the towering, iconic sculpture of Bangor, Maine's, mythical native son Tall Bunyan. (Better see a podiatrist about that one.)

No one knows where these misnomers came from, but they are catching. More than once I've accidentally told a friend that I'm going to "Old Ladies" (Old Navy) to shop for pants. However, I admit I was embarrassed that one time when Lindell said much too loudly inside a Staples, "You call this the Office Stupid Store?" and that other time when he told a room full of women that his mom wears a lot of "cow butts" (Talbots).

I remember when Owen, now 8, called yellow "ye-yo," and Ford said "God" instead of "dog." I also remember how Ford often elongated vowels that should be short (CONE-gress) and pronounced a word phonetically because he had only read it and not yet heard it said aloud.

These phases pass too quickly. Soon enough, Lindell will not mispronounce his Rs ("Pleston" instead of "Preston"), and he will stop saying "what" when he really means "that" ("Can I wear the shirt what has a puppy on the front?").

But the sad thing is, I probably won't hear these "lasts." Not really. No one stops to say, I bet this is the last time you'll do/say _____. Although I have carefully cataloged all the boys' first words (God, car, Spongebob), I might not realize the last time Lindell says Big Donald's instead of McDonald's. I might not notice the last time he says Tall Bunyan. These fleeting moments will slip by as unnoticed and unrecognized as the last time I carried Ford on my shoulders.

But every time I pass an L.L. Bean, I will always, even if momentarily, think of it as Yellow Beans.

ADS SET PARENTING BAR TOO HIGH

MY YOUNGEST SON, LINDELL (THE YOUNGEST OF THREE boys, remember) watches too much television. Granted, he's not in front of it all day long, but he watches more television than I ever allowed my oldest son, Ford, when he was 3 years old. (I also combed Ford's hair and wiped crumbs from his mouth before he left the house.)

Lindell's television habits do weigh on my conscience, though, even as I realize that it's sometimes necessary to occupy him while I do the 582 other things expected of me in a day. In this way, the third child often symbolizes the delicate balance between all your previous parenting philosophies and real life, which seldom comes from the pages of a parenting book.

Happily, those commercial-free, preschool-on-television channels are Lindell's favorite. This makes me feel better. After all, "Yo Gabba Gabba" does tell him not to bite his brothers ("Don't! Don't! Don't bite your friends!"), and without "Wonder Pets," how would he know what a pangaroo is? (Wait, what is a pangaroo?)

One day, Lindell was watching his favorite channel while I folded laundry. At the point in the show where there would have been a traditional advertisement, there was a public service announcement (I'm convinced) disguised as a Martha Stewart–like homemaking segment for kids. A mother and two children appeared on the screen. They were standing in a clean kitchen with fresh sunlight coming through the windows. I was only half-listening, but I knew what the mother was about to do. She was about to make me look like a bad parent. I might have dived for the controller to intercept, the way I sometimes do before an imminent profanity on my older boys' TV shows. But the controller has been lost for days.

The television mom announced the craft: frosting cupcakes to look like Dora the Explorer. Everything from the plaid valances in the background to the way the mother said "template" with a crisp accent emphasizing the "p" annoyed me. According to the instructions, children and their parents should melt chocolate, place it in a ziplock bag, and snip (there was that crisp "p" again) one of the corners to form a makeshift pastry bag. Next, the mother made an outline of Dora's hair with the melted chocolate. Her ziplock pastry bag never busted open. Nor did any chocolate spill out the other end and down the sleeve of her shirt.

Lindell watched with interest that bothered me. He didn't even move his eyes away from the screen when he reached into the bowl in front of him, picked up a goldfish cracker and stuck it in his mouth.

Sure, the craft looked easy enough—if you had someone buy the ingredients and set them on the kitchen counter for you in an orderly way. Oh, and also if your children calmly wait for instructions instead of sucking the melted chocolate out of the bag first. In the ad—and to be sure, this bit was selling something—the children didn't grab, whine, bicker or knock the bottle of food coloring onto the floor.

The segment was over in less than two minutes. But in that brief period of time, the producers had managed to change my son's perspective: Moms are supposed to spend their whole day doing crafts with their children, not studying for grad school, going to work, folding laundry, cooking dinner, or maybe, just maybe, having some free time for themselves. They were setting the bar too high.

Surely creators of segments like this know that firstborn children aren't watching it. No, firstborn children are actually doing crafts with their mother. It is second- and third-born children such as Lindell, the ones with moms who are spread too thin to consider crafts, who are the creator's captive audience. They also happen to be the same children who already have a chip on their shoulder about skinny scrapbooks and too many hand-me-down clothes. Playing on mothers' emotions through these children is like poking a stick in a fresh wound.

After the segment was over, Lindell looked at me expectantly. With his eyes he made his thoughts clear: "Shouldn't you spend the rest of your day doing that craft with me? Clearly other moms are doing it. I bet every other mother in this city is doing that craft right now."

I talked back with my own expressive eyes: "Look, kid, I'll call every mom I know. Not one of them is doing that craft."

At the next commercial break, there was another "ad" that announced, "We're not perfect, we're parents."

"Did you hear that, Lindell?" I wanted to say. "Huh? Did you hear that I'm not supposed to be perfect? Didn't I already take you to the library and on a walk? Didn't we just do 12 puzzles together? Don't I sing you to sleep at night?"

Thanks, children's programming, for pitting me and my son against each other. As if raising human beings wasn't hard enough.

About a Boy in a Kayak

Maine summers are beautiful, but so fleeting. Soon enough, the snow will fall and dark will come before dinner. Little wooden teepees will cover neighbors' shrubs, and stakes on the side of the road will mark how far the plows should go. And before Christmas Eve, we will begin dreaming of summer again.

This, by the way, is why I fell in love with Maine six years ago. For the first time in my life, I understood summer because I had felt the winter.

To mark the end of this summer, my son Ford and I did one of our family's favorite things: we kayaked out to the middle of the lake and watched the sunset. A few months ago, the sun was setting in a valley between two mountains. Now it has moved and is setting farther south. "The sun hasn't moved," my son reminds me. "We have."

Kayaking trips with Ford can be deep. He tells me about physics and how everything in the universe has mass—except for our thoughts, because technically they don't exist. (Is this why we value thoughts? Why we try to hold onto them?)

Watching a sunset with Ford is a cerebral affair.

On this particular night, Ford and I discussed time. It was our last week on the lake, after all, and school was looming in the distance. Also, Ford was worried we'd miss the sunset because dinner had gone late. It seemed like everything was on a schedule and clocks, real and imagined, ticked in our ears.

I told Ford that it's impossible to miss the sunset entirely unless you don't go out at all.

"That's not true," he said. "The sun actually sets at one precise moment."

I thought that over. The sun does dip below the horizon in one seemingly impossible second. You blink and it's gone. After a full day of hanging in the sky ("The sun doesn't 'hang,' Mom."), the sun slips behind the trees in one final movement. It's there, and then it's not. Kind of like summer.

Ford continued, "Everything in life happens at one precise instant. Nothing really lingers."

We debated this for a while. Is the sunset the moment the sun goes below the horizon? Or is the sunset everything leading up to that second, and everything after?

I think the best part of the sunset is after the sun has gone down. That's when light reflects off some clouds and casts shadows on others. The colors turn warm—orange, red, and sometimes purple. If the sky is just right, the colors can even cast a glow on people's faces.

"Yeah, but then the sun is gone," Ford said. "It's already set."

Suddenly, we both realized we were talking about more than a sunset. I was thinking metaphorically, about how the sunset reminds me of raising kids, and Ford was—well, Ford was still thinking about physics. But as the sky turned orange and Ford continued to talk, I thought about how many of the best things in life are fleeting. Raising kids is filled with so much emotion because it doesn't last. They grow up.

College is memorable because it came to an end. Our birth-days mark the passing of an age we will never see again. We long for our 20s because they went by so quickly.

And just like the sun, thinking back on these things after the precise moment they ended is sometimes the most moving part of all. After the sun goes behind the trees, you stare at the colors and forget that 10 minutes before, you had a headache from the glare.

Ford was silhouetted by the light as he circled my kayak and continued to talk about science. He's broader and taller now, but his face still has a glimmer of that little boy I once knew—the one who seemed to grow in an instant. I hardly remember anymore how loud Ford was as a baby, or how he always woke up early. I just have his baby face—laughing—engraved in my memory. It's the most beautiful vision.

But that's just a thought, and Ford said thoughts don't exist. Which is exactly why I pine for that little face, isn't it?

When winter comes, we will all forget the flies and mos-quitos of summer. Sunburns will fade and also be forgotten. We'll only remember moments like this, floating in a kayak, watching the sunset and listening to a boy talk about life.

Oh, Maine. Seasons come and go in a moment, leaving only the beautiful colors of a sunset in our memory. Until the next summer.

Because unlike most things in life—childhood, baby laughs, our 20s—that come and then are gone for good, we can all cling to the promise that another fleeting Maine summer will come again.

To Ford as He Begins High School

BEGIN WITH THE END IN MIND.

That's what the principal said at the orientation for next year's incoming high school freshmen. He was talking about knowing your goals and how he and the staff are dedicated to supporting and guiding you—our whole family, even—through the next phase of your education. But at that very moment, my mind went elsewhere, and I knew: I have done this all wrong.

I pictured your face the day we went to kindergarten orientation—your big brown eyes and toothy grin—and the way you eagerly explored your new desk and the pencil box filled with crayons. I remember it like it was yesterday. You had wanted a dinosaur backpack, but I couldn't find one, so you settled on a Tyrannosaurus rex shirt instead. Your hair was freshly cut, and when you sat at your desk, your shoes didn't even touch the ground.

No, back then, I did not have this end in mind.

I guess I believed you'd always be with me. For so many years, you were an extension of myself, always under foot or close behind. That's why I had to send you to public kindergarten, after all. Six full hours of not needing to answer "Why"? Yes, please! I couldn't wait for my free time (if "free time" is defined as staying home with your younger brother and being seven-months pregnant with another).

The morning of your first day of kindergarten, you came to my room and cried. You didn't want to leave me. You said you weren't ready and suggested that you stay home instead. You promised to watch the History Channel and read important books.

What I told you was, "You have to go because it's the law." What I was thinking was, I've been looking forward to this day since the moment you learned to talk and never stopped asking "Why?" Now, for six hours each day, someone else would have to answer why the Earth has only one moon, why dogs see only black and white, why light bulbs get hot, why Richmond is the capitol of Virginia, and why—

Wait, how did I not see this coming?

Your new high school is the best big "small" school we could imagine for you. Here you will be supported and excel. The principal will know your name and welcome you with it each morning.

But when I heard someone say "SATs" and "graduation," suddenly I realized what all this means.

And I'm not ready.

I don't want you to go. Not yet.

I looked across the auditorium at the high school staff. There were teachers from every field: English, science, history, French, art, music, math. I thought of all the conversations you'd have with them, how you'd talk for hours about World War II. Suddenly, I felt jealous. Those teachers get to be with you six hours each day. They will answer all your "whys." The coaches will see you in the afternoon. They will become your mentors, my partners in moving you closer to your goals.

Still, I will wait at the kitchen table and beg you stay.

I will never forget your red, teary eyes staring out the bus window as it drove away for your first day of school. We had never really been apart before that. But just as clearly as the moment is engraved in my memory, the image that haunts me regularly today, the one that can make me cry in an instant, is the one of you coming home on the bus later that afternoon. You stepped carefully down the large stairs of the bus, but once your feet were on the ground, you ran to me yelling, "Mommy! Mommy! I did it." You wrapped your arms around me and said into my shirt, "Do I have to go back tomorrow, Mommy?"

How did I miss this? How did I not notice the moment we went from you clinging to me, to me clinging to you?

As we toured the high school, people said how quickly these four years will pass. "Before you know it, he'll be graduating," they said.

I wanted to punch a clock.

I'm not ready.

In the beginning, I never really thought about this end.

Dad tells me that I should be happy you are growing up. Your best years, he says, are still ahead. How did I not know that my best years will always be when you were running through the grass to tell me about your day?

I imagined your graduation as I sat in the auditorium. Maybe you have, too. But I bet we see it differently. I bet you excitedly pictured yourself embarking on your own and starting the rest of your life.

Me? I saw myself waiting on the sidewalk, a pain in my heart, because I never wanted this time to end.

BASEBALL

BASEBALL SEASON IN MAINE

THE SNOW HERE IN MAINE IS MELTING. THERE IS ONLY ONE small mound of packed snow behind the garage and one next to the front sidewalk, where previously, for the past three months, there was a 4-foot wall of snow. We affectionately referred to this as the "Wall-O-Snow."

With a snowblower and shovel, Dustin and I in December cleared a path through the Wall from the driveway to the front door. When the boys walked through it, they couldn't see above the snow. It was like they were going through a corn maze. Sometimes my middle son, Owen, 6, would be afraid. Other times, he and Ford, 8, pretended the maze of shoveled snow was some kind of spaceship in *Star Wars*.

But now, sadly (surprisingly), the Wall is gone, and as the snow levels recede in our backyard, I'm discovering a virtual time capsule of lost toys, shovels and gloves. One by one, the forgotten items are unearthed as the snow melts away. Like counting the rings of a tree to determine its age, the layers of snow represent the preceding months and weeks. The top layer, which fell in January and February, reveals lost winter equipment such as blocks used to make snow forts. The bottom layer of snow contains even longer-forgotten summer items such as toy trucks, a sand shovel and Ford's baseball glove. It was the discovery of the baseball glove that was most poignant for me.

With the departure of winter comes the arrival of one of my favorite times of the year: Little League season. Maybe this is why God gave me only boys. If I didn't love the smell of red baseball dirt and the way it tints a new pair of white tennis shoes, and if I didn't love the sound of a baseball when it hits the bat or the feel of splintered bleachers, I'd be in a very sorry state as the mother of three boys.

As it turns out, watching my boys play baseball seems the perfect way to spend an afternoon. When I saw that the baseball park several streets over from our house is finally visible again for the first time since December, I knew that although we had our fun in the snow, we have more fun ahead of us at the fields.

Of course, being a mom in the bleachers isn't always easy. In fact, it's usually bittersweet. It takes a tremendous amount of "letting it go" to watch your child, possibly the one who is still afraid of the dark or likes his waffles cut up and with syrup on the side for dipping, step onto the field—or worse, disappear into the dugout—with a team of peers who may or may not taunt him for getting the first out or not making it to third base.

It is from the bleachers of Little League games that most mothers see the first glimmer of their boys becoming men. You know that he will likely cry into his arm in the car on the way home because he didn't hit the ball, but for now, he rushes to the dugout with his friends and throws his fist at the air in a very cool, darn-I-should-have-gotten-that-one sort of way.

You see him suck in his breath and set his chin in a de-termined point when the coach tells him to run faster, even as you know this is the same boy who wants one more bedtime story and one more hug before going to bed at night.

I suppose the emotional torture, if you will, of mothers at baseball is due to the fact that despite it being a team sport, your child is often singled out with all eyes on him as he goes up to bat. Sometimes I can hardly watch. My heart pounds. And not because I want my sons to be good, but because I want them to *feel* good. There have been many times that I was tempted to scale the chain-link fence, grab my child and tell him, "It's OK, honey, Mommy is very proud of you!"

This sort of behavior, of course, has been strongly discouraged by my husband, Dustin, who intuitively knows that babies become boys and boys become men on the baseball diamond. Doting mothers have no place in the process.

Yesterday, I picked up Ford's lost baseball glove, the one that the Wall-O-Snow spit out in its purge. The glove was right beside a toy airplane that had made him cry because it didn't work. I smiled, even as my heart slightly ached, to think about another season sitting in the stands, helplessly watching the slow unraveling of my boys' childhood, and, like the snow falling away to reveal hidden treasures, seeing glimpses of who they are to become.

First Day of Little League

There are certain images held in my memory like a snapshot. If my mind wanders over these pictures, I might spontaneously cry. So I keep them tucked away, and someday, when my children are grown, I know they (the images) will torture me.

Most of the pictures are of Ford, my oldest son. Ford and I have experienced and learned everything about parenthood together. I have failed him more than any of my other children simply because it was all new to both of us.

The first and most painful snapshot is of Ford's face peering out the window of the bus on his first day of kindergarten. He was crying. I didn't know what to do, but something told me that running onto the bus in my bathrobe to save him wouldn't make things better. So I just stood there and waved until the bus drove away and I couldn't see his face anymore.

The second picture is of Ford standing on the baseball diamond for his first night of T-ball practice. His new team jersey was too big and hung almost to his knees. This was a good thing because the pants hidden underneath were also too big and I had rolled the waistband over once to keep them in place.

Ford's face was red from crying. I had forgotten to pack a thermos of water and we brought the wrong baseball glove. Dustin, then a Navy flight instructor, was doing a night flight with a student, so I thought I was doing good just to get all three kids in the car with their shoes on. Ford's whining wore on me, and I yelled, "Stop acting like a baby." I immediately regretted it. Especially later, when I looked at him standing there on the field, and I realized that he really was a baby—my first baby.

The third image is from two weeks ago, on the night of Ford's first Little League practice. He hopped out of the van and ran across the parking lot. "See ya, Mom," he called over his shoulder. So different, I thought, from the days when I held his hand and told him to watch for cars.

I struggled to get Ford's brothers, Owen and Lindell, out of the van, as well as the bag of supplies (thermos, check; snacks for Lindell, check; ball for Owen, check), then the three of us followed several feet behind Ford. He was running ahead, his bat and glove held at his side. In front of him was the Little League field. The kids looked big. Definitely older, I thought. Must be the wrong field.

Suddenly Ford stopped running and turned around. He walked back to me and his brothers.

"Mom, those kids look really big," he said.

"That's because it's not your field," I said, slightly annoyed. We were running late. "Now hurry or you'll be late."

Ford jogged away from us again, the gravel crunching beneath his cleats. Then he stopped and turned around. His face was red. "They're very tall," he said, more frustrated now at my lack of understanding.

I was frustrated, too. "Because that's not your team," I snapped. "Those kids are much older. Now, seriously, keep running or you'll be late."

Ford breathed in and grunted. I had seen that look on his face before, like the time I packed the wrong glove and no thermos. He turned around and started running again, then he disappeared behind the concession stand, and for all I knew, he had found the team of younger, shorter kids. I hurried along with Lindell on my shoulders and dragging a bag behind me.

When Owen, Lindell and I finally rounded the concession stand and came into view of the other baseball diamonds, I saw what Ford already had seen. There were no other baseball teams. Those big, tall, older-looking kids were Ford's teammates.

Ford already was on the field. It was easy to spot him: He was the only one wearing white baseball pants and he was several inches shorter than the rest. I sat down on the metal bleachers and felt the lump in my throat growing. Yet I wasn't sure which made me sadder: the fact that Ford looked so much like a baby again, or the awareness that in another two years, he will be a "big, tall, older-looking kid."

I added the snapshot to my growing collection of images, the ones that I'll revisit when I'm older and ask myself: Did I do enough? Was I good enough? Do they know how much I've loved them? But mostly: When exactly did Ford—my first baby, the kindergartner crying on the bus, the Little Leaguer in baggy pants—grow up?

FATHER-SON MOMENT AT THIRD BASE

IT WAS THE TOP OF THE FIFTH INNING. THE WIND FINALLY had calmed down, except for an occasional breeze that threw pollen into the air. Because the sun was setting, the sideways light made the flying specks shimmer like fireflies. They flickered and rained down on the baseball field.

There were only a handful of games left in the season, his first in Little League. He still had not hit the ball. Dustin spent hours coaching him in the backyard. Through the screen, while I cooked dinner, I heard the rhythmic thump of the ball hitting the inside of their mitts.

"You ready to try batting?" Dustin would say.

"No, not yet, Dad."

More thumping.

"You afraid of getting out?"

"No, not really."

"Just keep your eye on the ball and swing."

"I know Dad, but —"

"You can't hit it unless you swing."

They went to the batting cage a couple of times for practice. And every night before and after dinner, they threw the ball in the backyard. Still, twice a week I sat in the stands twisting my fingers into the palm of my hand while he stood frozen at the plate, unable (perhaps unwilling) to swing. At some point, this became a metaphor to me: My son, who didn't stop wearing his Superman cape to preschool even after the other kids made fun of him, was now uncharacteristically unmoved by the opportunities flying past him. Where was the kid who told his first coach, "I've worked real hard all summer, and if you give me a shot at the infield, I think I can do it"? Where was the kid who once told me, "No one knows what you are capable of until they give you a chance"?

Well, he was there at the plate, paralyzed in the face of his peers, suddenly the victim of wanting to save face. He had taken off his cape.

Sometimes he was walked. Other times he was out, and I could see his small shoulders slouch as he walked back to the dugout.

Dustin never missed a game. While I chatted with other moms and made trips to the concession stand, Dustin stood like a lighthouse rising up from the ocean behind the fence near third base. He could not be moved. Often I saw them speak to each other with their eyes and movements. Dustin would swing a pretend bat in the air, reminding him to keep it level. Or he would point to his eyes as if to say, "Focus."

Still the bat never left his shoulder. He wouldn't swing. I grew frustrated, caught up as I was in the idea of the metaphor. But Dustin never lost patience. He never sighed. He just watched.

I had grown used to the routine: Here he comes to the plate; there he is frozen with fear; now he'll trot to first base or head back to the dugout; the crowd will politely cheer and say, "Nice try, kiddo!" So I almost missed it when it finally happened. He had two balls and two strikes. One more, and he was out. I tucked my camera back into its bag.

I looked up just before I heard the crack of the bat. It was a nice crack, too; the solid kind that comes from the center. The ball flew in the air to left field, past third base. No one looked more surprised than he. His eyes grew large and round as he watched the ball move dangerously close to the foul line. He ran to first base holding onto his helmet with one hand on his head. I stood and screamed, dropping everything from my lap. Then I leaned to Dustin and asked, "He did hit it, right? I didn't imagine it?"

Dustin didn't take his eyes off the field as he answered me. "Yep, he hit it."

When he got to third base, he was directly in front of us but facing the opposite direction. He leaned his hands on one knee, ready to run home after the next batter hit the ball. He looked over his shoulder, his dark brown eyes peering out from under his helmet. He didn't need to search; he knew where his dad would be standing.

Dustin gave him a thumbs-up.

He smiled back.

I always thought it would be me he looked for in the stands. (Well, at least until there was a girlfriend there.) But I wasn't the one at the batting cage, and I wasn't the one throwing the ball in the backyard. His dad was.

The bleachers were loud with excitement. Younger siblings played beneath the metal stands. People walked to and from the concession stand. And in the middle of all this commotion, a father and son shared a moment. It was a moment that didn't necessarily include me, but it is written on my heart just the same.

Where Have All the Baseball Kids Gone?

Each April, my older boys eagerly await the first phone call from their Little League coach. I'm probably biased, but he's the best one out there. For years he has continued to coach, even after his own son grew out of the league, and he has seen ballplayers go from too-young-to-play siblings on the bleachers to captains of the team.

This year, the call from Coach came while we were on our way back from a weeklong vacation in Washington, D.C. I put him on speakerphone so that the boys, in the back of the car, could hear. Their smiles were impossible to hide. The first practice would be in just a few days, the first game in a couple of weeks.

Ford and Owen wanted to know which new kids had been recruited for the team. They recognized some names, but not others.

And then the coach said this, "Two teams had to be cut this year. We just didn't have enough kids trying out. So the players from those teams went back into the draft, and some of them will join our team."

The boys looked confused: Two teams got cut? What?

For as long as Ford has been playing Little League, there have been six teams. Players stay with their team throughout the three to four years of Little League, and the team names have become a legacy. Older teenagers say, "Oh, I was on that team when I was a kid." Parents say, "I always wanted to be on that team." Younger siblings say, "I hope I get to be on that team, too."

"The league lost two teams?" Ford asked. "Why?"

"Not enough numbers trying out," Coach said again.

But two whole teams?

Ford and Owen were stunned. It was impossible for them to understand why boys all over the city aren't counting down the weeks until Little League's opening day. How could the league not have enough people trying out?

My boys are biased. They love baseball more than any other sport. But in the front seat, I was worrying about something else: Where have all the kids gone? It's not just Little League; on any given day, only a handful of kids are playing in the park down the street. Most of them have mothers hovering nearby. The sidewalks aren't filled with kids walking back and forth looking for a game or a neighbor to play.

And now our Little League can't fill up six teams?

This isn't a new concern. The term "Helicopter Parents" didn't come from nowhere. For quite some time, academics and sociologists have lamented the loss a childhood that includes a mother hanging out the door and screaming, "Come back when the street lights turn on!" The handheld-device generation has been absent from the outdoors for several decades now.

But Little League?

I thought Helicopter Parents wanted to involve their children in as many organized, after-school activities as possible. I thought the sidewalks and parks were empty because all the kids were at soccer, baseball and dreaded "play dates."

So if the kids aren't in sports, at the park or playing outside, then where are they?

This troubled me for several days, until it occurred to me that of course Little League would take a hit in this new generation. Baseball is one of the most hands-off (as far as parents are concerned) sports a child can go into. Everything about baseball breeds autonomy: the dugouts that separate parents and children, the fence around the field, the space between the outfield and the bleachers. (Go ahead and try to coach your child from the sidelines; they probably won't hear you.)

One mother told me that baseball is too much of a "time commitment," and that's why her son doesn't participate.

It's true; the teams practice for about two hours several times a week. "And the weekend games," this mother said, "they go on for hours!"

Okay, so games are long, but practice? Well, that depends on perspective. If you stay with your kids, practice probably seems long. If you drop them off, as I do, it doesn't seem long enough. I can hardly get through the grocery store and it's time to go get them again.

But that's only if I drive them. Most days, they walk to and from the field, and then I get a few extra minutes. A whole gang of boys travels down the sidewalk with baseball bags slung over their shoulders. Who knows what they talk about. Probably a continuation of the same no-parents-allowed talk that goes on in the dugout.

You see, besides the sport, all of this—the walks, the dugout, the team—is why my boys look forward to baseball.

Each spring, they get a little independence from me. They bond with a team. They go into the dugout as little boys, and they come out just a wee bit older.

And, well, I guess I'm surprised more boys—and moms—aren't signing up for this.

Last Year of Little League

Ford was 9 years old the day I dropped him off for his first Little League practice. He ran from the car with only his glove and a bottle of water, then he turned around and came back.

"I don't think that's my team," he said, pointing with his thumb at the ball field behind him.

I looked out across the playground and beyond the fence with yellow plastic on it. Boys who looked like small men were playing catch.

"They do look older, don't they?" I said. "But the coach said to meet here, and that's the field, so . . ."

Ford headed to the ball field again, a little slower this time. As I watched him go, I noticed his loose baseball pants and how his small, bouncy steps were still those of a little boy.

By the second year of Little League, Ford had grown an inch or two, but he was still the smallest on the team. Our league keeps players together and with the same coach for all four years, so Ford's teammates—the older ones, especially— were like mentors for him. The experience of Little League was as much about the game as it was time in the dugout.

On the field, what little experience Ford had was starting to show—from the way he handled the ball to his more confident stance at the plate. But he still missed more pitches than he hit, and he usually got on base by way of the other team's errors.

Ford began his third year of Little League with his younger brother Owen. It was an exciting season to be on the team. They won all but two games and went on to win the championship. Another highlight for Ford was when the coach asked him to pitch a few games. Physically, his shoulders were getting (just barely) broader, and he had outgrown some of his pants.

Ford began his fourth and final year of Little League with *Field of Dreams*-style aspirations. He was a team captain, one of the big kids—the ones who hit home runs or stole bases—that he remembered looking up to. But while some of his friends had already had their growth spurts, Ford was still among the shortest.

He had become a great fielder with "a soft glove," as one of the dads put it, and I no longer held my breath each time the ball came his way. I knew he would make the play. But he wasn't a big hitter. (A growth spurt probably would have helped with that.)

Ever aware that this was his last year, Ford went into each game with a growing sense of bittersweetness. After the last game, the coach called Ford up in front of the team. He choked on his words as he said goodbye to him, and tears made tracks down Ford's dirty face.

You probably wanted a happy ending for this, but there isn't one. Ford never hit a home run. He wasn't the hot-shot pitcher. And he still hasn't hit his growth spurt. What's worse: He didn't make the All-Star team.

These are moments we can't make better for our children.

Ford shut himself in his room that night, angry at the world. While I cried myself, I took out his first and last years' team pictures and looked at them side-by-side. At 9 years old, his big, eager smile said, "I can't believe I'm on Little League!" At 12, his tough-guy stare with only a glimmer of a smile revealed just how tumultuous and ambiguous these years must feel. Little League was Ford's boyhood, and now it's gone. As the oldest of three brothers, he has no one to show him what's next.

Yet, even though Ford has not reached his height, and he's stuck in the difficult place between being a boy and a young man, when I looked at those pictures, I knew he had grown in perhaps a more important way. He had just learned that we don't always get what we want, even when it's all we've ever wanted. He learned that life sometimes feels unfair and not everything comes easily. He had learned that wanting something and earning something are two different things.

And soon, I hoped, he would also learn that disappointment gets easier over time, and, if we let it, makes us more determined in the future.

MARRIAGE AND OTHER THINGS

Dustin Goes to a Civilian Dentist

Now that Dustin and I are living in Maine and out of our element (large Navy towns such as San Diego, Calif.; Norfolk, Va.; and Pensacola, Fla.), sometimes it feels like we are foreigners. We have never lived in a largely civilian town before, so we are navigating new territory, one without a squadron Spouse Club or military hospital, and no aircraft carrier in sight.

By far, one of the biggest adjustments has been the lack of a military hospital. For as long as I can remember, I have been treated by military doctors at military hospitals. Because of this, I have a child's understanding of health insurance. The first time I had to fill a prescription while on vacation and not near a military base, I felt like the pharmacist was speaking a foreign language. He wanted my insurance policy number, a guarantor and (gulp) a co-pay.

"Don't I just show you this [holding up military identification card] and you give me the medicine?" I asked.

Turns out, it doesn't work that way off base. There is paperwork, insurance cards and money (lots of money) involved. I was relieved when I returned to the familiarity of the military hospital, where all I need to know is my husband's "last four" (the last four digits of his Social Security number), and Uncle Sam takes care of the rest, including assigning me a physician.

When we moved to Maine and outside of any military treatment facility area, I had to find my own doctor. I felt like a college student picking a major. I was sure I would screw it up. I wanted my mom—or, at least, Uncle Sam—to help. How does one go about finding a doctor? It was harder than I thought.

Some doctors, in fact, fill up and quit accepting new patients. When one doctor's office turned me away, I wanted to cry like Richard Gere in *An Officer and a Gentleman*: "I've got nowhere else to go!" This doesn't happen within the bubble of the military hospital. The onus is on the military, not the individual, to make sure that everyone in the family has a competent doctor, their records are where they should be, and the doctor gets paid.

To be honest, if my 33 years as a military dependent is any indication, this type of system breeds complacency. Until now, I've never had real ownership of my own health care. It's scary—like jumping into the deep end without a raft—to be in control, but also liberating.

Yet, if I've been sheltered by military medicine as a dependent, Dustin has been even more sheltered as a service member. When we were in big Navy towns, Dustin didn't go to the hospital. The doctor—aka "flight surgeon"—came to him. Flight surgeons are feared by military pilots because they have the power to find you a new career path based on physical ailments. Pilots are notorious for not seeking treatment for fear that the flight surgeon will take away their ability to fly.

I forgot what an adjustment it would be for Dustin to see civilian doctors here in Maine, until he came home from a dentist appointment one day and could not stop talking about it.

"Did you know that you are supposed to brush in circles, not back and forth?" he said. "And look at this neat toothbrush the doctor gave me."

He treasured the tiny spool of complimentary floss that came with the free brush. That's when it occurred to me: Either Dustin's dentist is a very attractive female, or he's as giddy as a kid in a candy shop to see dentistry outside the beige cement walls of the military clinic, where it is not uncommon for them to yank out your wisdom teeth, pat you on the back, and send you off to work again.

Dustin has been simply indulgent, however, when it comes to his general doctor's appointments with the civilian physician here. Where once he would hide his headaches and stuffy ears from the flight surgeon, just this week he has seen his civilian doctor three times.

Yep, he's pretty much addicted to this quasi-civilian lifestyle.

I suspect we both are.

THE IMMORTAL COFFEE MUG

ADD A CERAMIC COFFEE MUG WITH A POORLY PRINTED IM-age of the Padres' stadium in San Diego, Calif., to the list of things that have almost destroyed our family.

In case you are keeping track, the tally looks something like this:

1. A *Star Wars* Tatooine skiff that everyone wanted and no one was willing to give as a Christmas gift and which now sits broken in pieces at the bottom of a toy chest, even after I learned that in its box, the skiff is worth the price of a small car.

2. The time that Lindell erased his brothers' progress on Super Mario Bros. Wii, and it seemed like the entire world had spun off its axis.

3. The Padres mug that I despise with the energy and fervor usually reserved for child molesters and arsonists.

We were planning a garage sale. Ever since relocating to Maine, we have kept a storage unit filled with all the boxes and knickknacks I was too exhausted (and scared) to go through before. Now it was time to purge. The portable storage pod seemed like a time capsule of our last few weeks in Florida. It was almost as if the fight Dustin and I had about packing the boxes too carelessly was preserved within the walls of cardboard. Its memory billowed out along with the smell of plywood, stored antiques and cardboard. On a bright, sunny Saturday morning, I opened the door of the pod, breathed in the smell, and was instantly mad at Dustin again.

But there was no time. Garage sale shoppers were already lining up on the driveway. I dragged out boxes of forgotten toys, baby items and wedding gifts (Tip: The cup and saucer sets that come with a place setting of china are totally worthless; register for a lawn mower instead). One of the boxes was filled with coffee mugs. There is only one person in our family who drinks coffee, and he only drinks it on Saturday. Therefore, one mug, in theory, should suffice. I put the other 24 mugs on the sidewalk to sell.

Enter Dustin, the rescuer. By that I mean he cannot bear to see the Waterpik flosser we've never used leave in the arms of another soul. During a garage sale, while I dicker with shoppers, Dustin runs around snatching items from people's hands and pleading with me about the usefulness of the broken hedge trimmer he was supposed to fix five years ago. He even rescues things not in the garage sale.

Shoes are the hardest for him to part with. He has about eight pairs of athletic shoes with varying degrees of grass stains on them and all with a different purpose: "I wear the blue ones to cut the grass. I wear the Nikes when I take the boys fishing. I wear the ones that my toes stick out of when I'm playing football in the backyard and there is a 30 percent chance of rain. I wear the black ones when the chance of rain reaches 70 percent." I have never known Dustin to throw or give away shoes when he buys a new pair. He just keeps them on life support and adds them to the collection.

There is one pair of shoes in particular that Dustin has rescued on multiple occasions. The heels are completely rubbed bare, the sole is separating from the fabric, and the insides smell like hot garbage. I threw them in the trash while Dustin was at work, and for weeks I thought the shoes were finally gone. About a month later, I opened the bottom of our corner cupboard and saw them there, like a hand reaching out of a grave. I shrieked at the sight.

Back to the garage sale. I went inside to get a drink and saw several of the doomed coffee mugs sitting on the kitchen counter. I took them back outside to sell. Hours later, they were inside again, this time hidden in the cupboard. I threw them in the trash. Dustin rescued the Padres one. I put it out on the driveway.

Dustin, who had grown panicked and presumably exhausted from all his search and rescue missions, turned to Owen, 7, and said, "Owen, please; don't you want to keep this coffee mug in your room? You could put pencils in it or something." Owen looked at Dustin, then at me. He grabbed the mug and ran cowering to his room with it.

I followed Owen, took the mug, and brought it back outside. With my eyes nearly popping out of my head and sweat pouring down my temples, I lifted the mug above my head and said to Dustin, "I have never hated a coffee mug so much in my life. I want to smash this all over the driveway."

"Sarah, it's just a mug," Dustin said. He looked scared.

Customers scurried to their cars.

I found the coffee mug in our pantry this morning. I am tempted to throw it away. But let's be real. Like Dustin's shoes, it's probably immortal. And I'm afraid to think which "grave" it might climb out of later.

Clean While No One is Watching

I AM SKILLED AT PURGING THINGS FROM CUPBOARDS, CLOS-
ets and basements. It's something I learned from my mom,
who has never been afraid to set a dumpster below a second-
story window and throw out armloads of junk. Mom doesn't
even sort through the piles. No, she plays like it's an extreme sport: How many pounds of junk can I throw out the
window without letting go of something I need? Mom will
even throw out the morning paper and your cereal if you
don't read or eat it quick enough. Her inbox is always empty.
Always.

Growing up with this, I developed a low tolerance for
clutter. Those reality television shows about hoarders are not
entertainment for me—they are a nightmare.

Five years ago, my skills were put to the ultimate test
when we moved from a 3,000-square-foot home in Florida
to a 1,500-square-foot one in Maine. I literally had to to
throw out or give away half of our things. And it was liberating. Living with less felt right.

Over time, however, the basement started to fill up again.
The boys' closets were stuffed. And one kitchen cabinet
door wouldn't close unless the saucepan handles inside were
delicately lifted up at an angle and held there until the last
second, when the door was latched shut. I have scars on my
wrist from this maneuver.

Last week, I couldn't take it anymore. It was time to clean, purge and reclaim space.

Naturally, I begged my mom to come up from Virginia to help me with this. Together, we are a formidable force. We can plow through piles like aggressively large lawn mowers that spit out grass clippings and chewed up leaves from the back. We don't rest until there are no more trash bags in the basement and the last load has been hauled off to the dump, recycling or Goodwill.

But Mom couldn't come to help me. I had to face it alone. Oh, sure, I have three sons and a husband to pitch in, but none of them—except maybe, Owen, 11—share my passion for emptying closets and drawers. In fact, everyone, except Owen, runs away when I bring out the industrial-size trash bags. If Mom is the ultimate organizer and I'm her protégé, my husband, Dustin, in particular, is her antithesis. Dustin is a rescuer of things and junk.

Regular readers might remember a column several years ago when I tried to get rid of Dustin's 4,000 (slight overstatement) coffee mugs at a garage sale. While neighbors and community members browsed our belongings strewn across the front lawn, Dustin followed close behind them and rescued all of his coffee mugs.

"That's not for sale," he said. One by one, he took everything that belonged to him and put it back inside our house. Only, he didn't find places for these rescued objects. He just left them on the floor and the kitchen counter. You see, Dustin doesn't really want to use those things again. He just wants to have them. It is for this same reason that we own knives that supposedly can cut through tennis shoes. Said knives do not, however, cut through the average tomato, and yet Dustin won't let me throw them out.

So, I did all my cleaning while Dustin was out of town. He would not see the boxes of coffee mugs and utensils leaving our door. He could not rescue anything.

My helper was Owen. Owen and I plowed through bins of old, broken toys and clothes that no one has worn. We purged the basement, the attic, the kitchen cabinets and everyone's closet. We sorted through winter gear, board games, DVDs and CDs. (Are you tired yet?) And at the end of the week, while the boys were at school, I took a load of filled boxes and bags to Goodwill. Any good cleaner knows it's important to get rid of the donations before past owners notice. One time, when I was getting rid of a talking puppy from Lindell's closet, it "barked" from the depths of a trash bag in the trunk of the car—and Lindell heard it.

"Is that my puppy? Is it in the car? Why would my talking puppy be in the car?"

This time, I rode to Goodwill in silence. There only was the occasional programmed voice coming from the boys' old *Star Wars* Millennium Falcon. A storm trooper hat made shooting sounds. A toy cash register dinged. I was getting rid of it all.

But when I opened the car door at Goodwill, suddenly it occurred to me: my boys' childhoods were in boxes and bags in the back of the van. Dustin's mugs laid at the bottom of a box.

My heart broke a little. Tears came to my eyes. I felt pangs of sadness and guilt.

Then I took a deep breath, steadied my hands, and threw everything out. Because, really, if I don't save us from "Hoarders," who will?

THE RAMEKINS

I'VE SAID IT BEFORE, BUT IT'S WORTH REPEATING: My military husband was trained for war and managing people who all have the same haircut.

This partly explains why he consistently takes the bottle of mustard from the condiments shelf but puts it back in the vegetable drawer or some other unlikely place. (More on this later.) It also creates trouble when he comes home and the children and I do not behave—or even think—like soldiers.

Imagine spending your entire workday with people who call you "sir," and then eating dinner with a 3-year-old who butters his roll with a spoon and has sideburns down to his earlobes. At the end of the business day, it is fair to say that Dustin leaves one planet and enters a new one.

Which isn't to say that Dustin and his "planet" are smarter than we are. They are a different kind of smart. Dustin went to the Naval Academy and has a degree in systems engineering. That doesn't mean he knows how to scramble an egg or navigate his Facebook account.

My Navy dad once was the captain of an aircraft carrier, but he still needed me to figure out his cell phone and beeper. In this way, it has been my experience that some of the smartest people (in the traditional sense) are the most clueless of ordinary things.

Take ramekins, for example. In case you are like Dustin, ramekins are small bowls with straight sides used for making certain desserts and side items. I use them to make individual chicken pot pies. One day, while I was preparing my recipe, I said out loud, "I wonder if I have enough ramekins for this."

Dustin was reading the newspaper at the table. He looked up and said, "I'm sorry, rammy-whats?"

"Ramekins," I said, my head deep inside a kitchen cabinet.

"I have no idea what you are talking about," Dustin said. "I've never even heard that word."

I came back out of the cabinet and stared at him. "But you've eaten out of one."

He looked confused. "It's something you eat out of?"

I found a ramekin and showed it to him.

"That's a small bowl," he said.

"No, it's a ramekin."

Later he asked, "Is the word 'ramekin' something that you deliberately learned? Did someone go out of their way to teach you that? Or is it just something you knew?"

He was sincerely concerned about the fact that he had made it to the age of 35 without knowing about ramekins. It's debatable which thing bothered him more: that he had never heard of a ramekin, or that I was keeping a "secret stash" of them in the kitchen.

Dustin was all caught up in the ramekin dilemma for several weeks. "Where do you learn these things?" he asked me several times. Apparently, for all of Dustin's intelligence, it is incredibly easy to impress him. You should see how smart I appear when I find his "lost keys" on the table beside the front door.

During this time, we had company several weekends in a row. Dustin asked all of them, "If I say 'ramekin,' what do you think of?" Most people thought it was a trick question. Their confused faces seemed to be saying, "Maybe 'ramekin' is an engineering term, too?"

On one of these occasions, we were actually eating out of ramekins. During dinner, Dustin said far too many times than necessary, "This ramekin is perfect for chicken pot pie." And, "Ramekins are so useful, don't you think?"

Again, our guests looked confused. Dustin was acting like an 8-year-old who has just learned the proper use of the word "sarcastic" and goes out of his way to fit it into a sentence. I mean, really, how do you build on a conversation about ramekins?

Then, last week, I asked Dustin to put some leftovers in the fridge. He got a casserole dish from the cabinet and said, "I'm just going to take this large ramekin here and fill it with some leftovers to be put in the fridge."

Ford, 9, said, "That's too big to be a ramekin, Dad. Ramekins are small bowls."

Dustin looked at me and said, "I give up. How do you all know these things? When did *he* learn what a ramekin is?"

I could see that Dustin needed to regain a degree of familiarity. He was like a foreigner in a strange land. He had tried to make sense of our world at home, and he had failed. After all this time, he still did not understand the difference between a ramekin, a bowl and a casserole dish. So I offered him some encouragement: "Dustin, why don't you go figure out why those ramekins retain heat so well." And then, because I knew that would not take him very long, I added: "Also, could you help me find my dicing mandoline?"

It's good to keep him on his toes.

Dustin Finds a New Way to Fly

I have discussed before how my husband, Dustin, while highly trained as a Navy pilot with an engineering degree from the Naval Academy, is not without his Clark W. Griswold moments. In fact, it has been my experience that the smarter a man gets in his profession, the more likely he is to fall off a ladder at home, drive away with his coffee cup still on the roof of the car or set fire to the kitchen.

Why do successful men have trouble functioning at home? I'm not sure, but I think it has to do with them not being able to multitask. Or maybe they use up all their smart energy at work. These are only guesses.

Just the other day, Dustin was doing what he calls the "car carousel," when one car in the driveway blocks another and he has to put the back one forward, and vice versa. His only task was to move the cars. It seemed like he could handle it. When I passed by the front window with a pile of clothes, however, I saw him step out of one car—now "parked" at the front curb—and run to the next one in the driveway. Only, he hadn't put the first car in park yet. Soon he was chasing it down the street and, I'm sure, cursing as he went. Once the crisis had been averted, Dustin looked up to see if I had witnessed it. I had. I gave him a smile and a thumbs up out the window. He spent an extra-long time outside after that, presumably because he didn't want to come in and hear about it from me.

To be fair, however, men also tend to cause problems for themselves, no matter how or where they've spent their smart energy. This seems to be part of their design. Their need to do all things fast, rough and with power tools only makes matters worse. And when two or more of these men get together, well, all kinds of trouble ensues.

When my family visited over Christmas, we went to a nearby hill to go sledding. The boys had just gotten brand-new, state-of-the-art foam "sleds" that actually look more like the boogie boards I was used to in Florida. But Dustin still insisted on bringing our old Radio Flyers, the ones I used when I was a child and are made entirely of wood and now-rusty metal.

The hill had a handmade ramp on it that had already helped many people catch serious air. The slope was also slick with ice. Still, this wasn't enough danger for Dustin. No, he decided that going down the biggest hill—the one with the ramp—with the Radio Flyer was the way to go.

Off he went in his ski pants from 10 years ago that are about 3 inches too short, two sizes too small and flatten his rear end like a pancake. He had on a full face mask, too. Dustin wasn't joking around.

At first, despite a running start and awkward belly-flop technique to mount the sled, Dustin didn't go fast. His ride started painfully slow. Then the sled hit a patch of ice and picked up speed. Dustin was going down the hill like an arrow, his body covering the child-sized sled like an elephant standing on a beach ball. Everyone at the top of the hill turned to look. "Is that an old Radio Flyer?" someone asked. I pretended not to know my husband.

When Dustin hit the ramp, he was catapulted into the air and did somersaults over the sled. All I could see was a ball of twisted navy-blue ski pants tumbling faster through the snow. At the bottom of the hill, Dustin pierced the snowbank like a splinter. Only his feet and his too-short snow pants were visible. The crowd made a collective "Ohh-hhh," then "Ouch" and "Oh, no."

But Dustin looked pleased with himself when he finally stood up and shook off the snow. I felt an urge to make apologies for him, to defend him to onlookers. "Really, my husband is usually very safe and smart . . . except for that time he left the keys in the car that wasn't in park . . . he probably looks smarter when he flies . . . maybe . . ."

Turns out, apologies and explanations wouldn't be necessary. For all of the shock expressed by people on the hill about this grown man about to go down the slope on an old Radio Flyer made for children, when Dustin got to the top again, a few men nearby asked, "Dude, can I have a turn now?"

You Can Take the Kid Out of Diapers, but Will Dustin Ever Hear?

We didn't need science to assure most of us that when compared to women, some men respond differently to interruptions from their children.

Scenario A:

Child: Dad, can I take the vacuum into the backyard?

Dad: Huh? What? Sure, yeah.

Scenario B:

Child: Mom, can I take the vacuum into—?

Mom: Nope.

No, we didn't need any experiments to tell us this is how it goes, but science has consistently backed up our claims anyway. Usually, however, the data relates to men and women's responses to babies.

After a 2013 National Institutes of Health study, the NIH "uncovered firm evidence for what many mothers have long suspected: women's brains appear to be hard-wired to respond to the cries of a hungry infant." These responses—mainly, interrupting focused attention—differed between genders but not between parent and nonparent participants.

In 2009, a British company called Mindlab, commissioned by Lemsip Max All Night Cold & Flu Tablets to study sleep patterns, found that the number one sound most likely to wake a sleeping woman is—yes—a crying baby. What did they find is most likely to wake a man? Car alarms, wind, buzzing flies, even crickets.

In a highly unscientific experiment over the holiday break, I discovered that these differences between men and women do not disappear—not in my family, at least—when the baby is out of diapers.

My oldest son, Ford (he used to wake me up by throwing his stuffed ducky against his crib mattress), has been reading Bill O'Reilly's Killing series—*Killing Patton, Killing Kennedy*, etc. His brother Owen (he never had to cry for me because I usually fell asleep feeding him) had given him one of the books for Christmas. Ford loves a new book almost as much as he loves a new phone, especially when that book is about history. Ford can't get enough history. In fact, his biggest pet peeve is that the History Channel doesn't really show history anymore. It's true. Flip to the History Channel at any point during the day, and you are more likely to see a reality television show than a documentary on Patton.

So Ford was super excited that "Killing Lincoln," the TV-version, would be on Fox News the week after Christmas. We talked about this many times. "Killing Lincoln" had become part of our daily conversation:

"'Killing Lincoln' will be on Fox News."

"Fox News? Isn't that a news channel? They do documentaries now?"

"It's a special."

"Are news channels becoming the new History Channel?"

"No, just look at CNN. It's mostly cooking and travel shows now."

"But 'Killing Lincoln' will really be on Fox News?"

"Yes."

The night the show would air, my youngest son, Lindell (he probably wakes up even the neighbors with his screams), started to worry that the show would be too scary for him.

"It's 'Killing Lincoln,' it's a book," we said. "It won't be scary. It's history."

Lindell ran around the room crying, "I don't wanna see 'Killing Lincoln'! I don't want to see 'Killing Lincoln.'"

Ford and Owen chased after him, mostly trying to reason with their youngest brother, but occasionally throwing insults such as "don't be a cry baby."

By this point, my heart rate had doubled. I did not dare take my blood pressure. I couldn't focus on my own reading. I couldn't even get the dishes done. I was referee, comforter and unofficial tally-person for how many times "Killing Lincoln" had been screamed in the living room.

Dustin sat on the couch reading the news.

"Aren't you going to help?" I said.

"Help with what? Those guys?"

"Yes."

"Okay. Boys, cut it out."

Lindell even jumped over Dustin's legs at one point. He sat next to him on the couch and beat his feet on the cushion, screaming "I don't wanna watch 'Killing Lincoln.'"

I brought out the O'Reilly books to show Lindell. I petted his hair that always sticks out on one side. I contemplated buying a second television to settle the fight.

And all the while, Dustin sat there and read the news.

Sure, to Dustin's credit, he had worked all day. Also, what's that word he uses? Oh, right—compartmentalization. Dustin's really good at compartmentalization.

But once I had finally settled everyone down, found the television remote and the right channel, my heart was beating like I'd just been in a fight. Adrenaline pumped in my fingertips. I sat with stiff posture, ready to grab the remote should, Heaven forbid, something scary actually come on the screen after I assured Lindell it wouldn't.

That's when the music for the special feature began. That's when the boys finally hushed and settled in for the show.

And that's when Dustin finally looked up and said, "Oh, wow, 'Killing Lincoln' is on Fox News tonight?"

DUSTIN DOESN'T LET ANYONE WIN

MY HUSBAND, DUSTIN, IS ONE OF THE MOST COMPETITIVE people I know. We've known each other since I was first born, but I only really came to understand Dustin's competitive nature when we were newlyweds. We were living in a small, one-bedroom apartment, and because we did not have children yet, we spent our evenings doing whatever we wanted. Sometimes that meant a spontaneous board game at 8:00 p.m. or a last-minute decision to go to the movies at 9.

Take note expectant parents. When people say "enjoy your flexibility before the baby comes," they mean it. Now is not the time to be looking through baby catalogs after dinner. Now is the time to do everything you won't be able to do again for 18 years.

On one of these childless nights, Dustin and I decided to play Monopoly. If you have also been married for more than 5 years, you know what a mistake this was. Newlyweds should play cooperative games, not Monopoly.

Here's the problem with Monopoly in particular: once you are losing, you can never come back. You are just filling a seat and taking your turns so that the winner can enjoy the remaining 4 hours of the game. Also, Monopoly is basically all luck. If you are the first person to get around the board and buy property, you will likely win.

This is where Dustin disagrees. According to him, "saving money and spending it wisely" means you'll win.

Related: I've never won at Monopoly.

So there we were, two newlyweds sitting down to a friendly game of Monopoly. Very quickly, I was losing and wanted to stop. But Dustin doesn't quit games either. Not ever.

"This is boring," I said. "Let's quit."

"You can't quit," he said. "That's like the worst thing I've heard you say."

So I continued to do my turns, despite imminent bankruptcy, and every time I landed on Dustin's properties, he charged me rent.

"But I'm your wife," I said. "You're really going to charge me rent?"

"In Monopoly? Yes."

That's when I cried and Dustin said he'd never play Monopoly with me again. Fifteen years later, he hasn't.

Right now, some readers are running to their computer to comment on my lack of sportsmanship. They'll say this little episode matches my personality—you know, the one they know of through print alone—perfectly. They will wonder if I'm teaching my kids to be sore losers, too. But you will know better than them because you have already read this far, and I'm sure you will read to the end, for the surprise ending.

Dustin has never let our children win either. To him, a game is not worth playing if you aren't going to play at your best. Whether he is playing basketball with the boys or teaching them how to play chess, Dustin has no mercy. Nope, not even when they are learning.

Dustin taught Ford how to play chess when he was 4-years-old, and he creamed him in every match. Ford still didn't fully understand the game, and his dad was beating him every single time. There were a lot of tears and frustration.

"Just let him win once," I begged. "It will keep him motivated."

"Actually," Dustin said, "letting him win will do the opposite. Why do you think he wants to play me every night? Because I win, and he can't wait to beat me."

Dustin even played Monopoly with the boys. Every time, he won. Owen still couldn't count money, and Dustin was charging him rent.

I have since bowed out of most family game nights. I sit in another room and knit while I listen to them argue. If I were to join, I might be tempted to give Lindell a loan, or let him magically inherit some of my real estate. And now I know that wouldn't help the boys at all. Here's why: When Ford was 12 years old, he came into the living room one evening and said, "I just beat dad at chess."

"That's nice honey," I said distractedly. "Good for you."

"No, Mom," he said. "Did you hear me? I BEAT dad. I did it. Eight years later, I beat him."

Dustin came out behind Ford. He had a big grin on his face. "The student has become the master," he said.

Ever since, Ford (and eventually Owen and Lindell, too) have known the true meaning of success. When it comes to challenging their father, nothing has ever been handed to them. They have earned every win.

Over the years, I've learned to revel in beating Dustin, too. I've won against him in Scrabble and Rummikub, and I'm still trying with Stratego.

So one day recently I said, "Let's play Monopoly. I promise, I won't cry this time."

Dustin laughed briefly. And then he said, "No."

"Afraid I'll win?" I teased.

"I've been married too long now to think playing Monopoly with you will be fun," he said. "Or that you will win."

Lost Wedding Band

I HAD ALREADY LOST A PIECE OF MY MARRIAGE, AND I didn't even realize it.

"What are they looking for over there?" I said to my sister-in-law, Megan.

Dustin and Megan's husband, Brett, were across the roaring brook, at the base of Mount Katahdin, staring into the foaming, churning water. Dustin had just finished riding a rope swing into the currents of what locals call Abol Pond.

"It's like someone lost something," Megan said.

Ten minutes later, Dustin came out of the water and motioned for me to leave the group and meet him across the rocky beach, in a secluded spot along the stream. He came close to me and held out his left hand, palm up. At first I thought he had a leech. Then I wondered if something was wrong with his hand. But when he pointed to his empty ring finger—misshapen and hidden from the sun for the last 12 years—I knew.

It wasn't that long ago that we passed a jewelry store in the mall and one of the employees offered to buff Dustin's wedding band. "I could get that ring shining like new," the man said.

Dustin said no. He was proud of the dents and scratches on his ring. It had been through many things in more than a decade: flight school, multiple moves across country, three children, deployments and a few near misses when

we thought it was lost forever. At a bonfire in San Diego, Dustin lost his ring in the sand. I cried that time, too. Then our friend Jamie, who had a beer in one hand and a plate of food in the other, ran his feet through the sand and said, "Is this what you're looking for?"

In the mornings, when Dustin had an early flight, I heard the familiar ping of his wedding band hitting the porcelain sink as he took it off before getting into the shower. Sometimes, he'd forget to put it back on, and the white-gold band, which had faded to yellow over time, would sit on the side of the sink for the rest of the day.

During flights and when he was on the aircraft carrier, Dustin kept the band in the zippered pocket of his flight suit. I wondered if he would forget it and what would happen if it went through the ship's laundry.

It never did.

Sometimes I held Dustin's ring on my thumb when he worried about losing it in the lake or down a drain. In movie theaters, I held Dustin's hand and rubbed my finger along the cold metal. The ring had been on his hand while he held mine during each of our children's births, even when my rings no longer fit on my swollen fingers.

It's true that Dustin's finger had grown around the band, and even when Dustin didn't have his ring on, the sun had made a de facto band in its place.

It was that white "ring" that I was staring at now, beside the river, at the base of Mount Katahdin, with tears in my eyes. Dustin went back into the water to search. I already knew it was gone. Yet he continued looking for more than an hour. The rest of our group left to get food. We would meet up with them later. Neither of us knew when to call off the search. At what point do you walk away? When do you feel satisfied that you did all you could do? If we left, we knew we'd never find it. But there was no hope even if we stayed. We couldn't walk away.

That's when it hit me. When a parent loses a child, how do they ever stop looking? When do they call off the search? How do they ever sleep?

Our three children were safe with their grandparents and aunt and uncle at a roadside market waiting for us. Was there any better symbol of our marriage than those three boys?

Dustin came out of the water one last time and hugged me. I cried into his shirt.

"I guess it's just a ring," I said.

"And I can't imagine a more beautiful place to leave it," he said.

We both looked out at Abol Pond. A group of white-water rafters screamed as they bounced along the roaring water. The sun was bright, the sky clear. Mount Katahdin was just beyond the trees.

"And anyway, I wear my ring here," Dustin said, pointing to his heart.

I knew we'd get him a new one before he leaves for his deployment. (That night, however, Lindell, 4, said, "Why does Dad need a new ring if he's not going to marry anyone else?" He has a point.)

A ring is just a symbol. I realize that. But as we drove away, I couldn't shake the feeling that I was leaving a piece of our marriage tumbling in the currents and bouncing off the rocks of Abol Pond.

Then Dustin squeezed my hand and I knew I was leaving with so much more.

New Wedding Band

This summer, Dustin lost his wedding band in the Penobscot River at the base of Mount Katahdin. I give him credit for keeping it as long (12 years) as he did. A person who regularly loses just one shoe cannot be expected to keep up with a 5 mm piece of gold. Interestingly, however, it took only one month for Dustin to forget that he needed a replacement. I seemed to be the only one with "get new wedding band" at the top of my to-do list.

Once the kids were back in school, we made a date of it. Naturally, memories arose of our first time. We were living in Pensacola, Fla., and we bought our rings at a small, local jeweler downtown. We had always intended to have them engraved, but depending on whom you ask, that never happened. (Dustin feels certain his first ring was engraved. Not likely since mine is not. But I'm not diving into the Penobscot to prove my point.) I remember eating Mexican food for lunch afterward and strolling down Palafox Street hand-in-hand.

Our second trip was not so leisurely. Lindell would be out of preschool by 11:30 a.m., and Dustin still had to go to work. Going to buy a wedding band seemed more like a necessity than an event.

We walked into the jeweler and found the case filled with men's rings. There, Dustin picked out what seemed to be the first thing he saw.

Let me backtrack and tell you that Dustin's old ring was completely ordinary. Dustin, you could argue, is ordinary. His closet is filled with striped shirts in various shades of blue. He never wears anything besides plain jeans (always the same cut; always the same shade of denim) or khaki pants. He has had the same brown leather belt since he was 21.

Going to buy shoes with Dustin is a mild form of torture. He tries on every shoe at every store in the entire city, deliberates for weeks, then, ultimately, ends up buying a pair that looks and fits exactly like his old pair. And he never throws anything away (well, except for his wedding ring). Rows of identical, old shoes line our basement and garage.

Because "you never know when you might need a pair of old shoes to mow the lawn."

Every Halloween Dustin wears the same costume: Where's Waldo.

So forgive me when I tell you that I laughed out loud at the ring Dustin first chose. It was thick, with squared sides and modern etching. The model on the poster was young, hip and dressed all in black.

"What, you don't think it's 'me'?" Dustin asked when he saw my shock.

I nudged him toward the style I knew—because I've been shoe-shopping with him—he'd ultimately end up with: The one that looks just like the old ring.

"Do you think those look like something I'd wear?" he asked.

"You wore one just like it for 12 years."

The salesperson measured Dustin's finger and slid the correct size onto his hand. Beads of sweat formed on Dustin's brow. His breathing was shallow. "I think it's stuck," he said.

He pulled at the ring, jamming it against his large knuckle, until the skin on his finger was red and swollen.

The salesperson assured him it was a good fit.

Naturally, I thought Dustin's struggle—his panic—was symbolic. I watched him suffer.

Once he got the ring over his knuckle and off his finger, he laid the band on the glass counter and said he could never wear anything like that.

Should have thought of that 12 years ago, Dusty.

The salesperson looked at me thoughtfully. Then she gave Dustin a ring one size larger.

That one was too big. Dustin was afraid he'd lose it.

Size, it seems, does matter.

Dustin was completely conflicted: "If I get the smaller one, what if my finger swells in the heat? Or if I get the larger one, what will happen in the winter?"

I reminded him that I've worn the same ring through three pregnancies and multiple stages of larger- and smaller-size clothing. I took off my band and showed him that my finger has literally grown around my rings. Indeed, my ring finger is quite deformed. Ring or no ring, I could never pass as single.

True, Dustin's finger has been spared the severe mis-shapenness that mine has endured. (Perhaps his old ring was bigger?) But it is contained just the same.

We bought the plain band and left it with mine to finally get engraved.

On the way home, I looked at my suddenly bare, disfigured finger. How long would it take for the skin to bounce back, to regain its usual shape? Probably never.

I looked at Dustin's hand—his smooth, symmetrical fingers—on the steering wheel and comforted myself with this: His are misshapen, too—if only metaphorically.

WEDDING BAND FOUND BY MAINERS

THE STORY I'M ABOUT TO TELL YOU IS HARD FOR SOME people to believe. After hearing it, they ask a series of predictable questions: You hired these people, right? You knew them ahead of time? Are you joking me?

However, because you are reading this in Maine, I trust that you, of all people, will simply smile and nod, knowing full well that this state is filled with incredible stories of people doing the most amazing things.

First, a little background. I met my husband, Dustin, when I was a baby. In fact, because my dad was deployed when I was born, I met Dustin seven months before I met my dad. Our lives intersected multiple times throughout our childhood, but for ten years, we didn't see each other at all. Then, when I was 20, Dustin and I went out on a date. We got married less than two years later.

On July 17, 1999, I gave Dustin a practical, inexpensive wedding band. He wore the ring every day for twelve years—through two cross-country moves, flight school, three children and two deployments—until July 30, 2011. That was the day we took the kids to Mt. Katahdin to visit our favorite swimming hole, an offshoot of the Penobscot River, where the water churns and a rope swing hangs from a tree. In three months, Dustin would leave for a yearlong deployment.

Dustin was swimming with the boys in the rapids when his wedding band slipped off his finger and disappeared into the foaming water. A wedding ring is just a piece of metal until that moment when it's gone. As I cried on the banks of the river, Dustin rubbed my back and whispered into my hair, "We'll buy a new ring before I leave, and someday, I'll come back here and find the real one."

But in my heart I knew: The ring was gone.

I wrote about the lost wedding band in a column a week later, and when Dustin left for his deployment that November, he had a new, shiny wedding band on his finger. But it wasn't the worn and scratched one that had represented our love for more than a decade.

Over time, I moved on and forgot about the ring.

Thirteen months later, in September 2012, I received a cryptic message in my Inbox.

"Hi Mrs. Smiley—My dad, Greg Canders, read your article about losing your husband's ring last year. My dad showed me the article this morning and we decided to attempt to find it. Could you please give me a call as we have found a wedding band and would like you to identify it. Zac Canders"

I hate to admit that at first I was skeptical. I had dark thoughts about Greg and Zac, whom I didn't know. Were they tricking me? Did they have some kind of motive? Did they want something from me? Because it didn't seem possible they could find the ring. And why would they look for it anyway?

I agreed to meet Greg and Zac at the Moe's Original BBQ parking lot in Bangor. Greg, a professional diver, told me that my column had touched him. In fact, he had saved the clipping and had it in his shirt pocket. That morning, he and his son had decided to drive 80 miles out of their way, with all of their gear, to find the swimming hole I had hastily described and look for the ring.

Greg reached into his other pocket and pulled out a small plastic bag. While my husband was still 8 time zones away, my hand trembled. Greg opened the bag and put Dustin's ring, tarnished and spotted from 13 months under water, in my palm. I slipped the ring onto my right hand.

Greg and Zac wanted nothing in return, though we had them to dinner, and Dustin could hardly wait to shake their hands. Three months later, he got that chance when he came home from his deployment. He held the ring with the same amount of awe that I had. But when I asked him, "It hardly seems real, does it?" Dustin said without hesitation, "I always knew we'd find it."

It's understandable when people can't believe this story. For me, however, besides being one more step in my and Dustin's long history, the lost-and-found ring, and Greg and Zac in particular, represent everything that I love about this state. Here, people do go out of their way to help others. People don't give up hope. And human connections mean more than money or fame.

Because of all of these things, while my husband continues to be away with the military, and I stay in our home in Maine, I keep the ring on my right hand, where it will stay until Dustin comes back to me again to wear it forever.

IF SCHOOLS WERE DESIGNED FOR INTROVERTS

IF YOU ARE AN INTROVERT AND YOU WENT TO SCHOOL, YOU know that our education system is not designed around you. Indeed, much of the world is not designed for you. The world is for extroverts, and the first time you learn this is your first day of junior high school, when the guidance counselor tells your class there will be "fun" after-school activities throughout the year.

You can't think of anything less fun.

In fact, if you could design the perfect school, it would look like this:

Cubicles in the lunchroom

The lunchroom would have the usual choose-your-own-adventure (or lunch mates) for extroverts, but it would also have cubicles for people like you. Because, for an introvert, there is nothing worse than that moment when you leave the lunch line, your tray in hand, and realize no one is going to tell you where to sit. You'll just have to pick the least crazy table and hope the people there will give you some personal space. You also hope no one will think you're weird for not talking. After a full morning of answering questions in class and working on group projects (the horror), you just need 20 minutes to yourself.

In the introvert's lunchroom cubicle, you could eat alone, in silence, without curious onlookers hoping someday you'll come out of your shell. You like your shell, thank you very much, and in order to go back out into the world (or, classroom), you need your quiet time there.

Lockers big enough to fit inside

At the introverts' school, every locker would actually be a portal to your own, private den of sorts. Hallways too rowdy and crowded? Step inside your locker and read a few paragraphs of your favorite book until the rush is over. Need to reflect on a comment someone made or a grade you just received? Step inside your locker for some personal reflection.

Also, all the talking and socializing that school necessarily requires is tiring for an introvert. It literally takes everything out of you. Step inside your you-sized locker for a quick nap to recharge your socializing battery.

One-man seats on the bus

Bus rides are a nightmare for most introverts. You're surrounded by all those extroverts who seem even more energized (what?) by their full day of socializing and being at school. You? You need some time to reflect and process, and sitting on a bus is the perfect place to do it. If you could just get some peace and quiet.

Not coincidentally, introverts' favorite seat on the bus is the random single-person one near the front. If introverts designed school busses, they'd make half the bus with single-person seats, all of them with a window so that you can stare at the passing scenery and think about your day.

A posted schedule for answering questions

As an introvert, you live in fear of the next time the teacher will call on you to speak in class. You can hardly learn because of all the brow-wiping you do wondering if the teacher will call on you next. What if you aren't ready to talk? What if you're having a quiet day?

At a school designed by introverts, teachers would have a published schedule for calling on students. No one would be called on without 24-hours advance notice.

Less team sports, more tennis, track and yoga

Physical education introduces many hurdles (pun intended) into an introvert's life. First, there is the locker room. Need I say more? Then there is the whole picking-teams thing. Introverts like to participate. They really do! But they don't need to be vocal about it. You won't find them jumping up and down after someone picks them for a team. Therefore, they don't get picked often.

No field trips, or the ability to opt out

Field trips are like the high dive for introverts. At least during a normal school day there is some structure. You go to one class and then another. There is a schedule. The teacher probably (hopefully?) even tells you where to sit in class. And then comes the field trip, which must be an extrovert's Disneyland.

Not only do field trips usually involve long bus rides (see above), but the extroverts of the world seem to go into hyperdrive over them. It's like someone fed them too much sugar. They are literally giddy over the idea of an unstructured, semi-spontaneous school day. There is very little personal space (no locker, no desk), and even lunch involves finding a park bench and listening to the overly excited extroverts again.

At an introvert's school, there would be no field trips or the ability to opt out of them. At the very least, if they're going to make you go on a field trip, they're going to have to give you some nap time in your locker afterward.

Fear of Flying

When people know that my dad was a career Navy F-14 pilot and that my husband is a Navy helicopter pilot, they are surprised to learn that I'm afraid—no, terrified—of flying. In fact, I've flown only once in my life, and that was in 1997. Dustin convinced me to go with him to Maui, Hawaii, where my two older brothers were living.

On a chilly December morning in Baltimore, Md., I sat in the airport lobby and watched the sun rise. Dustin had agreed to stay awake through the entire 14-hour journey so that I could ask him questions and perhaps, if I got scared, grip his hand hard enough to leave an imprint of my fingernails. However, after we had boarded the plane, and before it had taxied down the runway, Dustin, who has the annoying ability to nap anywhere and at any time, was fast asleep, his head resting on my shoulder.

Luckily, the flight was smooth and I felt like a seasoned traveler by the time we landed in Honolulu and took a smaller airplane to Maui. My brother drove us in his Jeep to the house he shared with my other brother, and I watched the sun, which had chased us all the way from Maryland, set on the horizon.

The whole experience was so pleasant, I almost forgot to be afraid when we boarded a plane a week later to return home. Then, somewhere over the United States, we hit turbulence, and the fear that rose from my stomach and turned my ears ice cold caused me to lose all inhibition. I sobbed like a baby and cried for my mom. Other passengers whispered to their children, asking that they turn around in their seats and stop staring at me, the spectacle in the back row. Dustin didn't sleep much.

Years later, when Dustin was deployed on the USS *Enterprise* and was scheduled for a port visit in France, he begged me to fly overseas and meet him there. I couldn't. If the turbulence en route to Baltimore had made me afraid, Sept. 11, 2001, sealed the deal. I had made up my mind never to fly again.

"Just take a sleeping pill and you'll never know you're flying," Dustin said. "I promise I'll find you in the airport and wake you up."

That didn't sound like a good idea to me. So while the other military wives flew to France to spend a week with their spouses, I stayed behind and offered to water plants, collect mail and feed animals in their absence. (Check out Chapter 12 of my book *Going Overboard*, and you'll see how well that went.)

Now it has been more than a decade since I last flew. Strangely, I love to watch airplanes, and I love being inside airports. But the thought of boarding an airplane is enough to drain the blood from my face. I can't explain my fear, and I don't expect you to understand it. (Trust me, my dad and Dustin have already told me all the reasons I shouldn't be afraid.) I also can't say whether my fear is based on being in an enclosed environment or being out of control, but I'm pretty sure it has at least something to do with being in a gigantic machine suspended in the air. In any case, my fear has caused me to miss out on family events, weddings, and even my grandfather's funeral.

Richard Lovelace, a 17th century English poet, wrote, "Stone walls do not a prison make/nor iron bars a cage." Ten years ago, I taught that poem to a fifth-grade class, and the meaning of the words suddenly struck me. Had I built my own wall-less, cageless prison with fear? The stanza became my mantra, even if reciting the words never actually propelled me into fearless action.

Then, in August, Dustin called me from work and asked, "How would you like to take a flight on a KC-135 with the 101st [an air refueling squadron with the Air National Guard based in Bangor]? They've just called and want to know if they can take you up for a ride."

Stone walls do not a prison make/nor iron bars a cage. Stone walls do not a prison make. . . .

Before I could stop myself, I said out loud, "Sure, I'll do it."

Just as my fear of flying is complicated, so is my decision to overcome it. When Dustin asked me about flying in the KC-135, my heart pounded in my ears, reminding me of being a kid, standing on the edge of the high dive and daring myself to jump. I had the same feeling when my brother took me up 110 feet to bungee jump—but he pushed me off the platform before I could back out.

On Tuesday, when I join the 101st as a passenger, I will finally jump for myself.

Flying with the 101st

Last Tuesday, 12 years after my first and only flight on an airplane, I was surprised to wake up feeling excited and adventurous, not afraid, about my ride in a KC-135 with the 101st Air Refueling Wing with the Maine Air National Guard in Bangor. Of course, I had to wake up earlier than normal for the morning brief, so maybe I was still half-asleep when my friend Sandy picked me up (Dustin volunteered to take the kids to school so that I could "focus"—on being scared?) and asked, "How do you feel? Are you nervous?"

"Not really. I feel great," I said.

My tone began to change, however, when we pulled onto the base and the runway looked like it was breathing snow. A white dusting, almost like a fog, rolled along the ground. I thought about the way my car behaves when I brake suddenly in the snow and tried to compare that to a tanker of not quite 200,000 pounds.

Suddenly, I needed to use the bathroom.

Several KC-135s parked near the runway rose from the mist of white like giant elephants standing in a line. I worried that the aircraft might fly like an elephant, too.

"All the snow will burn off by the time you fly," Sandy said.

I swallowed hard and went into the operations building where 15 other people were already seated in the auditorium waiting for the preflight brief.

It's important to note here that this event was not arranged specifically for me or the other passengers, a mix of city officials and spouses or employers of members of the 101st. The military does not spend taxpayer money frivolously, and nothing happens that doesn't support the overall mission. On Tuesday, that mission was a training exercise refueling a KC-10 in midair.

Occasionally, however, when there is a mission appropriate to the task, the 101st invites spouses and civilian employees aboard as a way of showing them some of what the members of the Air National Guard do. They also invite the media to help the public better understand what the 101st does. "[Our mission] is sometimes invisible and we need you to understand what we do," Col. Doug Farnham, the day's co-pilot, said during the brief.

That understanding is critical because the 101st is largely made up of traditional guardsmen and women who rely on civilian employers to work around service members' drill weekends and deployments. On Sept. 11, 2001, for example, 98 percent of the wing was recalled to the base within three hours. That amounts to hundreds of temporarily abandoned civilian jobs. Yet, as Col. Farnham noted, employers continue to be overwhelmingly supportive of the increased tempo of military responsibilities since that time. Public outreach, such as Tuesday's flight, certainly helps.

Dustin had arrived from taking the kids to school before the brief began. He sat in the seat next to mine and squeezed my hand. This moment had been a long time coming. After

12 years of encouraging me to fly again, Dustin finally was getting his wish. I knew that his excitement about sharing his life's passion with me was similar to the joy I feel when he experiences glimpses of my world at book signings and speaking events. Having me in the plane with him would be like me knowing Dustin is in the audience when I am onstage speaking.

The final brief was about safety. We were instructed on where to escape from the aircraft in case of an emergency and how to use the personal oxygen device, something similar to putting a Jiffy Pop bag over your head, if the cabin lost pressurization. My stomach was in knots. Dustin got up to find the bathroom while I struggled to contain my nervous laughter throughout the rest of the brief. While Dustin was beside me, I felt calm. When he left, I was nervous again. So I was relieved when I saw him return. It was almost time to board the airplane.

Dustin took a seat one away from mine this time and motioned for me to lean over to him. He whispered in my ear: "I just threw up in the bathroom." And then, because he knew what I was going to ask: "I'm not kidding."

I knew he wasn't. All three of our children had just recovered from the stomach flu. Dustin's face looked as pale and sweaty as theirs did over the weekend.

"I can't go on the flight with you," Dustin said. "But I'll be watching from the ground. I promise."

I felt frozen with fear. I was tempted to back out.

"You can do this, Sarah," Dustin said.

Soon after, Lt. Col. Kelley, my new best friend (you'll learn why next week), asked us to make our way to the bus that would take us to the KC-135.

Dustin hugged me tight and whispered in my ear that he was proud.

For a moment, I wished that it was me who had thrown up in the bathroom.

MISSION ACCOMPLISHED

ON DEC. 8, I OVERCAME MY BIGGEST FEAR BY FLYING IN AN airplane for the first time in 12 years. I was invited by the 101st refueling wing of the Maine Air National Guard, which likes to periodically take members of the media on board the KC-135 tanker to help the public better understand its mission.

Shortly before I boarded the plane, Dustin threw up in the restroom. It was our first indication that he had caught the same stomach flu our kids suffered the weekend before, the one I had secretly hoped to catch, because there's no better excuse for not flying than vomiting.

I left Dustin pale and clammy at the 101st's operations building and boarded the KC-135 with Lt. Col. Deborah Kelley, a petite blonde with a sassy bob hairdo and friendly eyes. I've been around plenty of people in uniform, but I've never seen anyone make camouflage and boots look so chic.

Also on the flight was Chief Petty Officer Eden Olguin, the NOSC Bangor command chief, who works with Dustin. I once saw him at a command picnic eagerly jump at what he thought might be a chance to go fist to paw with a bear. He eats crickets for snacks. He pulls the stingers off bees to suck their poison. If we had to parachute out of the airplane, my plan was to jump on Chief Olguin's back. Then I found out the KC-135 doesn't have parachutes.

Lt. Col. Kelley was surprised that the idea of parachutes had been a comfort to me, considering my fear of flying. I looked at the gray tanker, which rose up from the snow alongside the runway like an elephant, and decided she was right. Parachuting would not be my best option. I might rather wrestle a bear.

Here in Bangor, the KC-135 is a common sight passing over the Penobscot River, or coming in for landings, when its body seems to skate across the tops of the trees near Fourteenth Street School. The inside of the KC-135 is equally impressive. If commercial airliners are the loft-converted-into-entertainment-rooms of large jets, the KC-135 is the unfinished basement. Our seats were red netting hung from the sides. The floors and walls were bare of any concealing plastic or luxuries. (There are no lap trays on the KC-135.) Overhead, the wiring is exposed.

You'd think that a large military jet with such transparency would scare someone like me. Yet the opposite was true. I have never seen wires so carefully bundled and labeled. Every inch of the airplane was immaculate. In this way, the inner workings were visible to the point of being reassuring.

Plus, I was sitting alongside many of the people who have worked on the aircraft for decades. The pride and confidence they have in their work were similar to a surgeon effortlessly, but knowingly, making his way around the operating room.

I sat directly behind the pilot and co-pilot on takeoff. Incidentally, since 1997, the only other time I've flown, I've had a recurring dream about being in the same spot, and just as the nose of the airplane begins to lift, I tell the pilot I've changed my mind and want to get out.

I thought of that dream as the KC-135 barreled down the runway. Surprisingly, however, I was not afraid. I saw the cool confidence of the pilots' hands and put my faith in their ability. When the nose lifted and we began to climb, I felt incredibly relaxed. The gravity and acceleration pushing my lap into the seat on takeoff reminded me of the same relaxing heaviness of lying in the hot sun. The aircraft slipped smoothly into the clouds.

Later I had the opportunity to lie on my belly in the boom pod at the back of the airplane and watch a KC-10 approach, like a kitten coming to its mother's belly, for mid-air refueling. By the time the two airplanes made contact by way of the boom, they were so close that when I waved to the other pilots, they saw me and waved back.

By the end of the three-hour flight, I was steady enough to sit and finish the daily crossword puzzle. I even yawned a few times. Lt. Col. Kelley cheerily offered me goldfish crackers from her bag. I felt like a seasoned traveler.

Indeed, the only mishap of the morning came when I had finished using the restroom. Unbeknownst to me, until I was already seated again, I had dragged a strip of toilet paper down the aisle of the plane. It wasn't stuck to my shoe. Worse, it was lying conspicuously on the floor. Do I get up and claim the toilet paper by putting it in the trash? I wondered. Do I leave it there and risk looking like a bad guest?

Just then, over the roar of the jet's engines, Kelley whispered, as best she could through the protective plugs in my ears, "Don't worry; I've got it." She stood, and in one deft, discrete motion, rid the floor of my errant toilet paper, proving once again that the military takes care of its own like family.

Would the people on a commercial flight do the same for me? I honestly don't know. But I'm not yet ready to find out.

FLYING: LET'S TRY THAT AGAIN

AFTER NEARLY 17 YEARS OF AN ALL-CONSUMING FEAR OF flying that left me grounded, I got on a plane in July with my husband and flew to Washington, D.C. I even flew back without Dustin.

I thought I was cured. So did Dustin. Nothing unusual had happened during either of the flights in July, besides the fact that I cried like a baby and gripped the armrests until veins popped out of my hands. But I had taken the first step, and that was the most important thing.

So Dustin and I scheduled another trip to D.C. in August. I would be flying with my husband both ways this time, and it seemed I had little to fear anymore. I still cried on the flight down, and, like last time, I worried about the flight home the whole week. But I always thought I'd do it.

When I woke up the morning of our return flight, my heart was pounding in my chest. I ate breakfast with the familiar hum of anxiety in the back of my mind. I felt sick to my stomach.

Still, I thought I'd actually fly.

The airport was busy because it was Labor Day weekend. I mentally sank into myself, the way I always do when I'm nervous or afraid. Dustin made hopeful small talk that I was too consumed to hear, and he reminded me how in less than two hours, our boys would be waiting for us at the airport.

He never thought I'd back out.

We got on the tram that would take us to the CRJ-200 waiting on the tarmac. Two children, who were traveling alone, were crying in the backseat. This got my heart rate going again. I thought about my own children crying, and my mind went to very dark places.

Still, I thought I'd fly.

Once I was buckled in my seat on the airplane, I lowered my forehead to my knees, and Dustin rubbed my back. The flight attendant noticed us and came over to make sure everything was okay. The two children were still sniffling and crying behind us.

"My wife is afraid of flying," Dustin said. "But she'll be fine."

"Would you like to meet the pilots?" the flight attendant asked. "Sometimes that helps."

I unbuckled and followed the flight attendant to the front of the small airplane. I really wanted this to help. But when the pilots turned around, they looked like they were 20. I didn't see any grey hairs or tough skin from years of shaving. My throat went instantly dry.

"It's going to be a great flight," the captain said with a boyish grin. "There's some bad weather ahead, so it will probably be bumpy, but . . ."

I turned around, pushed Dustin aside and ran down the steps to the tarmac. I didn't care that my purse and computer were still inside the aircraft.

Nearby, airplanes were starting up their engines. It was loud and windy on the ground. Dustin came down the steps, and I could see that he was frustrated—maybe even panicked. For the first time, both of us realized that I might not do it.

"Get on the plane," Dustin yelled over the noise of the other engines.

"I can't."

"Just get on the plane, and we'll be home in 2 hours."

"I can't do it."

I was hysterical now, and other people on the plane were beginning to peer out their windows. If there were any other anxious fliers that day, I'm sure they were tempted to run, too.

One of the pilots came out and asked if he could help. He wanted to explain the principles of flight to us.

"I'm a pilot," Dustin said exasperated. "And so is her dad."

The pilot looked confused. Then he asked if there was anything else he could do. I wanted to say, "Get about 20 more years experience and take back what you said about rough weather."

When the pilot left us again, Dustin said, "We're getting older, Sarah. Everyone is going to look younger to us—our doctors, dentists, the children's teachers."

But it didn't matter what he said. I couldn't get back on the plane.

Dustin retrieved our bags and without saying another word (for about an hour), rented us a car and began driving me home. Our plane landed safely in Bangor before we had even gotten outside of D.C. traffic.

Anxiety: it's a rotten thing to deal with. It never really goes away, and it's hard to explain to anyone who hasn't experienced it. My fear is irrational and inconvenient. I know that. And this week, on the anniversary of 9/11, I also know what I eventually have to do: get back on a plane and reclaim my independence.

FAQs about Failed Flying Attempt

I hate to say that I'm glad "I'm not the only one," because it means that others have suffered from anxiety and phobias, too. But reactions to last week's column about my failed attempt at flying in an airplane have made me feel somewhat normal. (Okay, maybe not "normal," but not alone either.)

Turns out there are a lot of fearful fliers out there. There's even people like me, people who think they can't get on a plane at all. Although, honestly, very few people self-reported leaving the airplane just before taxiing down the runway, as I did over Labor Day weekend.

Some readers wanted more information—to make themselves feel better or to laugh at me, I don't know. I'll try to answer those questions below.

What did security think?
The security personnel at Reagan International Airport in Washington, D.C., were definitely startled, and perhaps on high alert, when I ran off the plane, but all of them were incredibly understanding as well. On the tarmac, when Dustin yelled over other planes' engines for me to get back on the plane, a baggage handler thought he was screaming at me. The man pulled me aside and asked, "Do you feel safe going with this man?"

"My husband?" I said. "Yes. I just don't feel safe in that airplane!"

Now the man had a clearer picture. I wasn't a hysterical wife; I was just hysterical in general.

"I see this at least once a week," he told me. "Really, it's going to be okay. When you go back to the terminal, there will be people waiting there to help you."

For a moment I wondered: "Will they be people in white coats?"

But, as it turned out, the man felt so sorry for us, he followed us back to the terminal himself to help us retrieve our luggage. We were too late. Both suitcases were already on their way back to Bangor. I hope they weren't scared.

How can you be afraid of flying if your husband is a pilot?

I don't have a good answer for this. Remember, my dad was an F-14 pilot, too. I've been around aviation my whole life. In fact, I love airplanes. I love to watch them land and take off. For one of our first dates, the one where I fell in love with Dustin, he took me to Gravelly Point, just across the water from Reagan International Airport, to watch jets screech seemingly just out of reach and land in front of us.

But I never wanted to get in those airplanes.

Maybe I've heard too much about flying. I've witnessed friends dying in training accidents while Dustin was in flight school. I've heard all the stories.

But then, a phobia is never really rational, is it? So even if everyone I knew was a pilot, it wouldn't have any effect.

How mad was Dustin?

To quote Dustin, me running off the airplane was the "worst thing" I've ever done to him. If that's the worst thing I've ever done to him, then I think I'm doing pretty well, don't you think?

Still, he didn't talk to me for at least an hour in the rental car.

But Sarah, you would have been safer in the airplane than you were in the car.

But the car doesn't fly suspended in midair.

Have you tried any programs?

I like to follow pilot Patrick Smith's columns, and I've read his book *Cockpit Confidential*. Seven years ago, when I backed out of a family wedding due to my fear, I even talked to Smith on the phone. By that point, unless it was Smith piloting the plane, I was still afraid.

I also frequent Capt. Tom Bunn's Fear of Flying website and online forum. These sites are helpful for making me feel less weird, less alone, but, again, unless Capt. Bunn is my pilot, it's like starting at square one when I get to the airport.

Is it turbulence, claustrophobia or a fear of crashing that scares you?

All of the above.

No, I take that back. Capt. Bunn and Smith have convinced me that turbulence can never hurt an airplane. Not really. And to be honest, I don't think I've ever experienced turbulence.

So, actually, my fear is mostly of the fear itself.

Trust me, you do not want to sit next to me on an airplane. I cry and hyperventilate. I rock in my seat and startle at every sound. It's miserable. And probably my biggest fear of all is not being able to do anything about it. I just have to sit there and feel the fear until the pilot lands the plane.

Actually, no; this is just what I tell myself.

I'm really afraid of crashing. Is anyone not?

Will you ever fly again?
With enough medication, I hope so.

ONLINE COMMENTERS

LAST MONTH, A LOCAL RADIO SHOW INVITED ME INTO THE studio to talk about online commenters. This meant that I had to (1) read through months-worth of online comments, and (2) still look in the mirror without feeling fat, stupid, ugly, and arrogant afterward. Because that's how some commenters describe me.

Commenters have a lot of things to say about everything—from my headshot to my parenting. And, really, that's fair. After all, I write publicly about my life. But let me clear up just a few misconceptions.

I Have Two Sons
I have three sons. If this is news to you, you are in good company. Many readers think I have only two children. Some commenters, in fact, accuse me of loving just two children and forgetting the third. They say I have favorites.

Much of this confusion stems from a national Eggo waffle shortage that happened many years ago, after which one of my boys seemed to disappear. That's right; you aren't imagining it. You're not crazy.

In the wake of the national Eggo shortage, I wrote about how many frozen waffles I've made since becoming a mother and how many more I'm projected to make before my children leave home. Readers, by the way, were outraged that I serve my boys frozen waffles for breakfast—even after I pointed out that I cook the waffles first.

But no one was more outraged than one of my sons, whom I described as flopping on the floor after learning that we didn't have waffles—that in fact, all America was out of waffles. He came home from school, slammed the door and said, "Never write about me again."

And I didn't.

Until a few years later when he said, "Why don't you ever write about me? Don't you love me?"

That son's name is Owen. He is my middle son. He has approved this message.

My Husband Must Hate Me

There is a common refrain on the comment boards, and it goes something like this: "Geez, why does this Dustin guy stay married to Sarah anyway?"

You know, I had never really thought about it. Why do any of our spouses stay married to us? I decided to ask Dustin.

ME: Why do you stay married to me?

HIM (without looking up from the newspaper): Because you make me less boring than I would be otherwise.

So, there you have it.

I'm Coddling My Children

These comments are my kids' favorites. They laugh about them as they walk home from school in cold, blowing snow. Then they laugh again when they call me and ask, "Can you come pick us up?" and I say, "No."

I'm Too Hard on My Kids
I'd respond to this if I didn't think these comments might actually be from my kids.

My Children Should Run Away
One of my favorite comments complimented me on "almost" admitting that I'm a "total failure" as a parent. I mean, at least the person gave me credit for something.

Another commenter suggested that my children should run away while they still can. And several years ago, a reader actually wanted to report me to Child Protective Services for the egregious act of letting my kids ride their bikes on a residential street.

Well, you can all relax, because Lindell did try to run away a few weeks ago. He took the dog, Sparky, and a handful of grapes with him. They got as far as the corner and came back. And this proves that being my child is at least better than living on the streets with a dog and some grapes.

I'm Hiding My Age with Old Head Shots
When a friend brought this comment to my attention, I grew a new wrinkle from laughing. Oh, how I wish I could use my head shot from 14 years ago. But it's really awkward to meet people in real life if your headshot hasn't aged right along with you.

The picture you see here today was taken in September. However, to be completely above board, I should tell you about all the aging that's happened since then: I have a new age spot on my cheek; a funny mole was removed from my left arm, and now I have scar; I have new gray hairs that are getting more difficult to cover; I can't see the small writing on a pill bottle; and, more disconcerting, I can't see my eyebrows to pluck them.

There, I think we are all caught up.

LESSONS FOR THE FUTURE

I'M NOT GOOD WITH NEW YEAR'S RESOLUTIONS, BUT THIS time of year has always made me reflective.

Question: What causes more reflection than the beginning of a new year?

Answer: Living with teenage children.

Until my older sons hit the ages of 12 and 13, I stumbled through my life blissfully unaware of all the embarrassment I had previously caused. I thought I was cool. I thought I was smart. I thought I understood computers. I thought no one noticed that I wore slippers to the gas station in the morning.

Now, each year, I become exponentially more like a caricature of myself.

So I won't pretend to be a better Sarah in 2015. While I still have teenagers at home, the cards are stacked against me. All I can do is look back at 2014 and try to glean some hints about how to be less of an embarrassment in the year to come. These include the following:

I will not drop off the kids at school wearing my slippers and bathrobe.

If I do wear my slippers and bathrobe to take the kids to school, I will not get out of the car.

I will canoe more and ride in the boat less.

I will actually paddle the canoe and not pretend while my kids paddle in the back.

If I choose to fly somewhere, I will in fact get on the plane. I will not choose to fly somewhere.

I will not cry during Little League games. I will not cry during *The Bachelor*. I will not cry at any time that might embarrass my teenage sons.

If I cry, I will pretend I'm laughing.

At 4:30 on a Monday in June, I will go outside to play and remember that in six-month's time, it will be dark and cold.

At 4:30 on a Monday in December, I will hunker down on the couch and remember that in six-month's time I will be mowing the lawn and pulling weeds.

I will remember that I don't actually mow the lawn or pull weeds anymore, and I will be glad that I have sons old enough to do it for me.

When I am tempted to fuss with the boys' hair or collars, I will pet the dog instead.

I will remember that the key to my son's heart is through roast beef and scalloped potatoes.

I will lie on the dock until the first stars appear and not say anything about the mosquitoes or bats.

I will not be afraid to put on a bathing suit.

I will not allow pictures of me in a bathing suit.

I will remember that before I rake the snow off the roof, I should always shovel the front steps first. No, wait! I mean, I will shovel the steps and then rake the roof. Right; steps first, roof second.

I will remember that the person taking my pizza order doesn't necessarily want to hear about my day or why I'm ordering pepperoni this time instead of Hawaiian.

I will step away from the chocolate chip cookies (and leave more for the kids).

I will invite more people to dinner (and serve them roast beef and scalloped potatoes).

I will not make up words to songs or create rhymes about the chores my kids should be doing.

I will not dance. Not ever.

I will not put notes with X's, O's or hearts in lunch boxes.

I will not complain when I lose in Monopoly.

I will not play Monopoly.

I will not make the soldiers in Axis & Allies talk to each other. I will not give the Monopoly pieces names. I will not feel sorry for chess pieces. I will not anthropomorphize anything.

I will remember that trying to make Mario do the moonwalk across a cloud does not constitute "playing Wii."

I will refrain from using my family member's pet names in public.

I will remember that taking my boys to any craft store, knitting shop, or boutique is not "quality time."

I will not sing at the grocery store, post office, library, Target, in the car, in the canoe, in the house or out of the house.

I will not—not in a million years—forget how wonderful, witty, smart and helpful my Lindiddy, Owey, and Fordy-Pie are.

ABOUT THE AUTHOR

Sarah Smiley is the author of a syndicated newspaper column published locally in the *Brunswick Times-Record* and *Bangor Daily News*, and in Washington, Florida, Colorado and Texas. Sarah has written three books: the memoirs *Dinner with the Smileys*, *Going Overboard*, and a collection of essays titled *I'm Just Saying* . . . .

She is a frequent contributor for *Parade*, *Huffington Post*, and Military.com. Sarah has been featured in the *New York Times Magazine*; *O, The Oprah Magazine*; *Parade* (cover story); *Good Housekeeping*; *Newsweek*; *DownEast*; *Maine*; and *Military Spouse* magazine (cover story). Sarah also has appeared on the *Today Show*, *Katie* (Couric), *Nightline*, CNN's *American Morning* and *Sunday Morning*, CBS's *The Early Show*, Fox News *Studio B*, and MSNBC *Live*. Locally, Sarah is a frequent cohost and guest on WVOM, *The Voice of Maine*, and *The Nite Show with Danny Cashman*. Sarah has been featured on WCSH6's *207* and MPBN. In 2014, Smiley was awarded the American Legion Auxiliary's prestigious "Public Spirit Award." She lives with her husband and kids in Bangor, Maine.